FROM PROMISE TO CONTRACT

Liberal theory of contract is traditionally associated with the view according to which contract law can be explained simply as a mechanism for the enforcement of promises. The book bucks this trend by offering a theory of contract law based on a careful philosophical investigation of not only the similarities, but also the much-overlooked differences between contract and promise. Drawing on an analysis of a range of issues pertaining to the moral underpinnings of promissory and contractual obligations, the relationships in the context of which they typically feature, and the nature of the legal and moral institutions that support them, the book argues for the abandonment of the over-simplified notion that the law can systematically replicate existing moral or social institutions or simply enforce the rights or the obligations to which they give rise, without altering these institutions in the process and while leaving their intrinsic qualities intact. In its place the book offers an intriguing thesis concerning not only the relationship between contract and promise, but also the distinct functions and values that underlie contract law and explain contractual obligation. In turn, this thesis is shown to have an important bearing on theoretical and practical issues such as the choice of remedy for breach of contract, and broader concerns of political morality such as the appropriate scope of the freedom of contract and the role of the state in shaping and regulating contractual activity. The book's arguments on such issues, while rooted in distinctly liberal principles of political morality, often produce very different conclusions to those traditionally associated with liberal theory of contract, thus lending it a new lease of life in the face of its traditional as well as contemporary critiques.

From Promise to Contract
Towards a Liberal Theory of Contract

DORI KIMEL
New College, Oxford

WITHDRAWN

·HART·
PUBLISHING

OXFORD AND PORTLAND, OREGON
2005

Hart Publishing
Oxford and Portland, Oregon

Published in North America (US and Canada) by
Hart Publishing c/o
International Specialized Book Services
5804 NE Hassalo Street
Portland, Oregon
97213-3644
USA

Hart Publishing is a specialist legal publisher based in Oxford, England.
To order further copies of this book or to request a list of other
publications please write to:

Hart Publishing, Salter's Boatyard, Folly Bridge,
Abingdon Road, Oxford OX1 4LB
Telephone: +44 (0)1865 245533 or Fax: +44 (0)1865 794882
e-mail: mail@hartpub.co.uk
WEBSITE: http//www.hartpub.co.uk

British Library Cataloguing in Publication Data
Data Available
ISBN 1–84113–212–8 (hardback)

Typeset by Hope Services (Abingdon) Ltd.
Printed and bound in Great Britain on acid-free paper by
MPG Books, Bodmin, Cornwall

to my parents and my sister
and
to Joe Strummer, the coolest and greatest

Contents

Acknowledgements

Through his work, as a D. Phil supervisor, as a colleague and as a friend, Joseph Raz has been an indefatigable source of inspiration and support. I cannot begin to put into words my affection for him and my gratitude.

Many friends and colleagues have provided me with insightful comments and queries on chapters and earlier drafts of the book. I am particularly grateful to Lizzie Barmes, John Cartwright, Nitsan Chorev, Anne de Moor, Julie Dickson, Ronald Dworkin, John Gardner, Grant Lamond, and John Stanton-Ife.

Material based on parts of Chapter 5 was published in 'Neutrality, Autonomy, and Freedom of Contract' (2001) 21 *Oxford Journal of Legal Studies*, and material based on parts of Chapter 4 was published in 'Substantive Rights and Remedial Rights in Contract Law' (2002) 8 *Legal Theory*.

My girlfriend Jocelyn Alexander has contributed enormously to every aspect of this book and to every aspect of my life during work on this book, to the extent that I cannot imagine what would have happened without her.

Introduction

ARE CONTRACTS PROMISES? When one philosophical question occupies generations of thinkers, all failing to come up with a conclusive answer, the suspicion arises that something is wrong with the question itself. I am not suggesting that this is necessarily the case with the opening question. There may be nothing intrinsically wrong with asking whether contracts are promises, just as there need not be anything intrinsically wrong with the question of whether a Jeep is a car. Clearly there is sufficient similarity between car and Jeep, contract and promise, to render such inquiries plausible. The problem, however, lies with posing these as 'yes–no' questions, expecting hard and fast 'yes' or 'no' answers. In both cases such answers, whether in the positive or in the negative, are bound to breed distortion. In both cases a more satisfactory answer would have the form of 'yes, but . . .'—or 'no, but . . .'—with the more illuminating bit being whatever comes after the 'but'. A Jeep, to pursue the simpler case, possesses some characteristics that all cars possess, and can fulfil most of the functions that cars are normally expected to fulfil and are generally capable of fulfilling. But a Jeep also possesses certain characteristics that cars do not normally possess, and is capable of fulfilling certain functions which are not normally attributed to and cannot normally be fulfilled by cars, and that at a price in terms of its proficiency in fulfilling certain functions that cars typically do fulfil. A complete analysis of the conceptual relationship between car and Jeep must not eschew such complexity. The same goes for the more intricate matter of the relationship between legal and non-legal practices that is at issue in this work.

'Legal theorists', Joseph Raz wrote, 'often create the impression that there are only two possible conceptions of the law of contract. Either its purpose is to enforce promises or a certain class of promises . . . or it is a hybrid of principles of liability based on torts and restitution, disguised so as to make their true nature obscure.'[1] My aim in this work is largely to offer a third approach to the question of the relationship between contract and promise. If pressed, I would classify my view as a 'yes, but . . .' (rather than a 'no, but . . .') type of answer. The reason for this is threefold. First, the parallel between contracts and promises—both facilitate and regulate (part of) the normative consequences of voluntary undertakings of obligations to others—serves as the starting point to my discussion of promise and informs many of my subsequent observations. Far from arguing against the notion that either contracts or promises can be characterised in such terms, much of my argument is intended to provide this

---

[1] 'Book Review: Promises in Morality and Law' (1982) 95 *Harvard Law Review* 916 at 933.

familiar view with further support. Secondly, theories of the 'contract as promise' variety, and particularly Charles Fried's modern rendition of the theme, have been, I believe, generally more satisfactory, or perhaps less unsatisfactory, than their alternative in the shape of a sweeping denial of the correlation between the two practices. Indeed, the reason for this may well be that the similarity between contract and promise illuminates at least as much, if not more, of the nature of contract as do the differences between them—and this may remain true even with regard to those differences which have been largely overlooked and on which I hope to shed some light. Finally, the 'contract as promise' school of thought has been customarily identified with the liberal tradition of contract analysis. And my view, although significantly different from what is commonly known as a liberal theory of contract (both in terms of the kind of liberalism by which it is underlain, and in terms of its understanding of the contract-promise equation), is intended as a development of this very tradition.

I mentioned Charles Fried as a notable advocate of the 'contract as promise' approach. For much of his career, Patrick Atiyah has established himself as per-haps the most forceful critic of this approach, and the most celebrated propon-ent of the kind of alternative view delineated by Raz in the above quotation. Yet in the same year Fried's *Contract as Promise* was published,[2] Atiyah, in his *Promises, Morals, and Law*,[3] added his voice to those who view contract and promise as analogous institutions. It must be said, though, that Atiyah's is no ordinary 'contract as promise' theory, for the path he took into the rival camp consisted in turning promise into what he had always argued contracts were—or, more accurately, were *not*, namely independent sources of obligation—and the methodology he followed along this path, that of using contract law as a basis for the analysis of promise, suggests that his approach should in fact be labelled 'promise as contract' rather than the other way round. Now it has been suggested (and I agree) that of the two it is Fried's endeavour which was the more successful, for whereas his analysis of contract law is (as I shall argue) based on an essentially sound understanding of promissory logic and seems strained mainly as a matter of explaining certain contract law detail, Atiyah fol-lows a questionable methodological formula on the way to an altogether counter-intuitive and far from convincing account of promise. Yet despite the striking contrast between their respective efforts, Fried and Atiyah can be seen as grappling with the same basic difficulty: that of reconciling apparent (and, as I shall explain, inevitable) discrepancies between promissory logic and contract law reality.

The very existence of such discrepancies, and the difficulties encountered by those purporting to reconcile them, can be taken to reinforce the case for a theory that recognises not just the similarity but also the disparity between the normative foundations of contract and promise. Yet I do not intend to invest-

---

[2] C Fried, *Contract as Promise: A Theory of Contractual Obligation* (Cambridge, Massachusetts, 1981).

[3] PS Atiyah, *Promises, Morals, and Law* (Oxford, 1981).

igate such discrepancies directly, nor expose as an end in itself the failings of known attempts to reconcile them. Mine is a positive argument to the effect that the similarity of function and value between contract and promise is but partial. As such, it does not depend for its validity on the existence of incongruity between certain aspects of the common law of contract (or the law of contract in any other jurisdiction) and promissory logic—an incongruity that, it should be recognised, could play but an evidentiary and in any event inconclusive role in this context. After all, the law itself, and not only the theory purporting to explain its normative foundations, can in certain respects be flawed, or without being flawed can incorporate to some extent (as it surely does) certain principles beside promissory ones even inasmuch as the latter lie at its heart. I do believe, however, that a more complete account of the relationship between contract and promise can provide a superior basis on which to explain some features of the law as it is, and on which to offer solutions to problems that it fails to resolve or resolves unsatisfactorily. Some such issues will be addressed in the later parts of this work, once the main theoretical argument has been set out.

I will start with an account of the normative foundations of promissory obligation. My aim here is, rather than to do full justice to the network of intricate philosophical quandaries this topic comprises, to set the stage for a comparison of promise to contract. Hence the special attention I will pay in this context to issues such as the normal background conditions for promising, the main functions this practice is suitable for fulfilling and the main values it possesses, and, in particular, the role reserved for trust in the promissory arena. Hence also my choice of Fried's analysis of promissory obligation as the starting point for this discussion.

The second chapter can largely be described as a detour, but one that will hopefully bring us back to the main road better equipped to face the rest of the journey. Here I will examine a thesis that was recently offered as a critique of HLA Hart's analysis of the way in which the law, and criminal law in particular, purports to guide behaviour. This discussion will provide me with the opportunity to explore a number of pertinent issues, such as the role of threats and coercion in the law, the relationship between these and trust, and the concept of trust itself.

In the third chapter, the focus of attention shifts to contractual relations. Drawing on earlier discussions as well as on an examination of certain features of personal relations in general, I will here introduce my main arguments concerning the similarities and dissimilarities between contract and promise. From there I will move on to examine, in the final two chapters, several issues arising in and around contract law. I will discuss, first, a number of problems concerning remedies for breach of contract, and, secondly, one familiar and one less familiar theme pertaining to the broader issue of contract law's positioning in the framework of liberal political morality, namely the freedom of contract and the freedom *from* contract. Through the final chapters' discussions I intend to illustrate some of the practical implications of the theoretical steps taken up to this point, and in the process put into context and thus further elucidate the main arguments which were made along the way.

Finally, I would like to mention two issues that cannot be addressed directly in the confines of this work, but on which it may nevertheless have some bearing. The first is the economic analysis of contract law, and the relationship between this type of scholarship and a project such as mine. In a recent survey article on the philosophy of contract law, Jody Kraus described what he calls 'philosophical' contract scholarship (essentially, for him, theoretical analysis of contract outside the economic analysis of law school of thought) and 'economic' contract scholarship as 'two bodies of scholarship [that] have largely passed each other like ships in the night,' only rarely and irregularly taking notice of each other.[4] Though this work is by no means a conscious effort to facilitate a happier or a more interactive future for these two bodies of scholarship, it is possible that its main theses are capable of at least diffusing some of the tensions between them. My arguments to the effect that the similarity between contract and promise is but partial, and in particular the thesis according to which (by contrast to promise) the intrinsic value of contract derives from this practice's ability to facilitate not personal relations but personal detachment, may have the side-effect of creating more room—if you like, more philosophical or even more moral room—for the application of economic considerations both in the descriptive and in the normative analysis of contract law. It is possible, that is, that what I shall describe as (valuable) personal detachment is an environment the creation and maintenance of which are matters far more accommodating to brute economic analysis than are the kind of inter-personal relationships that form the environment in which promissory logic resides.

The second issue is the relationship between contract law and other—in the eyes of some competing—legal disciplines. It is not new for contract law to come under pressure as a discipline upon whose very distinct existence doubt is thrown. The main candidates for bringing about the death of contract are tort law (into which contract law could allegedly be absorbed or re-absorbed, as argued in Grant Gilmore's celebrated work[5]) and, more recently, the law of restitution, the emergence of which as a legal discipline unto itself could allegedly render contract, again, as a sub-category holding no particular interest within a much broader legal field. Of course, a complete refutation of such views necessitates not only the analysis of contract, but also the corresponding analysis of that discipline or those disciplines that supposedly threaten contract's distinct existence. Yet my endeavour on the one hand to disentangle (to some extent) contract from promise and, on the other hand, to bring to light contract's unique functions and value, could, if successful, substantially improve contract's chances of survival when the more comprehensive inter-

---

[4] JS Kraus, 'Philosophy of Contract Law' in J Coleman and S Shapiro (eds), *The Oxford Handbook of Jurisprudence and Philosophy of Law* (Oxford, 2002) 687.
[5] See *The Death of Contract* (Columbus, 1974).

legal-disciplinary contest is embarked upon. Contract law's distinct and independent standing, that is, is much more likely to withstand such challenges when the practice's unique functions and value are seen for what they are, than as long as it is understood as either a not altogether successful or consistent version of promise or a haphazard amalgam of disparate principles of liability.

The systematic exploration of these two issues will have to await another day. For the moment, let us stay with promise, contract, and what is between them.

1

On the Nature and Value of Promises

━━●━━

T HE NORMATIVE FOUNDATIONS of promises, and their role and value as a
social practice, have been explored by generations of philosophers, political theorists and social scientists. My aim in setting out to add a few drops of
my own to this ocean of literature is relatively modest. My comments are
intended as a basis on which to study the relationship between promises and
their alleged legal equivalents, contracts.

This narrowness of aim explains a few things about the discussion that will
follow. It explains, notably, my focus on what I shall describe as the normal conditions and circumstances for promising, as opposed both to necessary conditions, and to circumstances in which or purposes for which the practice may be
used but which are, in one sense or another, marginal, esoteric, atypical. For
although such matters may be of significance for the study of promise per se, it
is the practice's normal function and mode of operation which should serve as
a basis for its comparison to contract.

My ultimate interest in this comparison also explains, in part, why I see fit to
use Charles Fried's account of the normative foundations of promise as a starting point for my discussion. His *Contract as Promise*[1] is the most celebrated and
probably the most influential modern defence of a thesis by that name, power-
fully continuing a theoretical tradition from which my work at the same time
draws inspiration and seeks to depart.

But there is another reason to launch the discussion with a look at Fried's
account of promise: it is, excuse the pun, a promising starting point. I see it as
such for two related reasons, both a reflection of what may be described as the
'Kantian' spirit of his argument. One, as I shall soon explain, is the strictly
'backward-looking' quality of his account of the binding force of promises.
Secondly, and more specifically, his argument touches on what I believe to be the
theme which holds the key not only to the nature and value of promise but, in
particular, to the analogy—and, as this work is largely dedicated to establishing, dis-analogy—between promise and contract.

This theme is trust. Yet Fried's succinct account of promises incorporates,
rather confusingly, *two* distinct themes: trust and convention. I will start with

---

[1] C Fried, *Contract as Promise: A Theory of Contractual Obligation* (Cambridge, Massachusetts,
1981) (henceforth *Contract as Promise*).

an attempt to disentangle the two, calling into question the significance of the latter before further exploring the role and the significance of the former.

Fried's Argument: Convention, Social Practice, Trust

Classified in terms of the distinction between backward-looking and forward-looking normative argumentation, Fried's account of the binding force of promises clearly belongs to the former category.[2] He explains the requirement to keep a promise as arising primarily out of the very act of promise-making, rather than from the consequences that breaking or keeping a promise may entail (eg increasing or decreasing the sum of happiness or utility[3]) and, for that matter, regardless of the immediate side-effects of the making or the breaking of a promise (eg, respectively, reliance by the promisee, unjust enrichment by the promisor[4]). Indeed his account may be said to be looking strictly backwards, not even sideways.[5]

Having established that forward-looking arguments fail to elucidate the notion that promise-keeping is a *general* requirement,[6] and that sideways-looking arguments concerning the binding force of promises are circular (unjust enrichment, reliance, occur precisely because promises are assumed to be binding[7]), Fried suggests that the way forward consists in recognising what he calls 'the bootstrap quality' of the required, backward-looking, argument: 'To have force in *a particular case* promises must be assumed to have force generally.'[8] The paradoxical appearance of this proposition, he continues, evaporates once the conventional nature of the matter at stake is recognised. He goes on to describe promising as 'a very general convention,' and, more importantly, one that serves highly valuable ends.[9] And from here, '[i]ndividual obligation is only a step away.'[10]

Let us pause for a moment and clarify a preliminary point. Promising can be said to be, or involve, a convention in two distinct senses. First, there is the thesis according to which there are linguistically conventional means *by which* to promise, that is, by which to communicate an intention to undertake, by that very act of communication, an obligation.[11] If we understand conventions as

---

[2] For the distinction, see B Williams, *Ethics and the Limits of Philosophy* (Cambridge, Massachusetts, 1985) 8.

[3] See *Contract as Promise*, at 15–16.

[4] *Ibid* at 9–12.

[5] The terminology is again borrowed from Williams, above n 2.

[6] Above n 3.

[7] *Contract as Promise*, at 11–12. For a similar argument see also GJ Warnock, *The Object of Morality* (London, 1971) 99–101.

[8] *Ibid* at 12 (italics in original).

[9] *Ibid* at 13. Fried's account of the value of promising will be examined at a later stage.

[10] *Contract as Promise*, at 16.

[11] This formulation is borrowed from Raz. See 'Promises and Obligations' in PMS Hacker and J Raz (eds), *Law, Morality and Society* (Oxford, 1977) 210. An earlier account which influenced Raz's view as well as some of my comments on the subject is GJ Warnock's, above n 7, ch 7. For a powerful defence of an alternative, reliance-based, view of promising, see DN MacCormick, 'Voluntary

solutions to co-ordination problems, then the co-ordination problem linguistic conventions of this kind (eg using the words 'I promise') are a solution to, is *how to communicate* such an intention.[12] Then there is the thesis according to which the very practice by which people undertake obligations through acts of communication in which they state their intention to do so, regardless of the linguistic means used for this purpose, is a matter of convention. Here the co-ordination problem would be how to achieve whatever it is that the practice as a whole is thought to be a means of achieving.

Fried does not clarify which thesis he has in mind when describing promising as a convention. The first thesis, however, though correct, seems patently irrelevant for the purposes of explaining the binding force of promises. The availability (in a given linguistic community, or culture, etc) of conventional means for promising could probably make it easier—simpler, quicker—to make a promise. But it would be a different matter altogether to argue that whenever such means are available (or let alone regardless of whether or not such means happen to be available) it is impossible to promise in non-conventional ways, or that the normative implications of a promise made by conventional means would be any different from those of a promise made by non-conventional means. Fried does not provide an argument to such an effect, and I cannot think of one either.[13]

But what about the second thesis? I have already mentioned one characteristic of conventions that does not square easily with promises: conventions are solutions to co-ordination problems. As through promising a person purports to commit herself in a special way to a certain course of future action—purports to make it her obligation—promises can sometimes be said to facilitate a form of co-ordination between promisor and promisee;[14] but even as such they can hardly be described as a solution to a co-ordination *problem*, classic examples of which are what side of the road to drive on, or who should call back when a phone conversation is unexpectedly cut off. Such problems involve situations where all participants have a common interest in opting for one course of action out of several (at least two) alternatives, with the interest in uniformity greater than the reason, if any, for preferring any particular course of action to its alternatives. It seems

Obligations and Normative Powers,' Supp vol 46 *Proceedings of the Aristotelian Society* (1972) 59; and see Raz's response, 'Voluntary Obligations,' there, at 79.

[12] The classic account of conventions as solutions to co-ordination problems, to which Fried alludes specifically, is David K Lewis, *Convention* (Cambridge, Massachusetts, 1969). There may be conventions which are not solutions to co-ordination problems. In a recent article, Andrei Marmor argues that this is the case with 'conventions constituting autonomous practices' ('On Convention' (1996) 107 *Synthese* 349). This type of convention is not pertinent, however, to the analysis of promises, and at any rate is not what Fried has in mind in his discussion. I will therefore continue, for present purposes, to use 'convention' in the Lewisian sense.

[13] A similar point was made by Raz in his critique of Atiyah's view. See 'Book Review: Promises in Morality and Law' (1982) 95 *Harvard Law Review* 916, at 927 (and n 21, there).

[14] And perhaps between promisor and third parties, too, subject to the possibility that the promisee, but not others and not necessarily to the knowledge of others, could release the promisor of her obligation.

very doubtful that promising is a solution to a problem with regard to which the predominant interest is uniformity of action, and even more doubtful that it is only one of several alternative solutions, so that the case for (uniformly) opting for *any* such solution is greater than the case for preferring a particular one.[15]

Other, related features of conventions, appear to be equally at odds with the practice of promise, and Fried's argument does not address such difficulties.[16] But perhaps we should not dwell on those either. All that Fried says about the social function of promises and on the basis of his understanding of it, touches on the notion that promising is, simply, a social practice. His account of the nature and the value of promising as a social practice has little do with the question as to whether the practice is conventional, and the argument he builds around this account depends little, as far as I can see, on how this question should be answered. More to the point, Fried's argument would be helped little by a positive answer to this question. From here on, accordingly, I will consider Fried's argument concerning the binding force of promises as an argument not from convention, but from social practice. How does it fare as such?

The value of promising as a social practice, according to Fried, lies in the way in which it enables participants to make use of the 'remarkable tool' which is trust.[17] Promise is '[t]he device that gives trust its sharpest, most palpable form.'[18] An important truth is captured, I believe, in this assertion (to which I shall return later); but let us concentrate for the moment on how this builds up, in the framework of Fried's argument, to an explanation of the binding force of promises. He believes, as we have seen, that it is necessary to understand promising as a social practice in order to come to terms with the 'bootstrap quality' of the argument. And the 'one step' that needs to be taken from here in order to meet that challenge is as follows:

> An individual is morally bound to keep his promises because he has intentionally invoked a convention whose function it is to give grounds—moral grounds—for another to expect the promised performance. To renege is to abuse a confidence he was free to invite or not, and which he intentionally did invite. To abuse that confidence now . . . [amounts to] the abuse of a shared social institution that is intended to invoke the bonds of trust.[19]

The argument, however, is not intended to derive its force from the notion that to break a promise is to abuse, and thus possibly *undermine,* a beneficial social institution. Since it is the case that to promise is to invite the promisee to trust, and in this sense 'to make himself vulnerable,' and that to break the

---

[15] For a detailed analysis and examples of co-ordination problems see Lewis, above n 12, at 5–24 (and see Marmor's comments, above n 12).

[16] Eg the point of individual compliance depending on the assumption of general conformity. See *ibid.*

[17] *Contract as Promise,* at 8.

[18] *Ibid.*

[19] *Ibid* at 16 (footnote omitted).

promise is to abuse that trust, the promise-breaker, he maintains, *uses* the promisee. Accordingly:

> The moralist of duty . . . sees promising as a device that free, moral individuals have fashioned on the premise of mutual trust, and which gathers its moral force from that premise. The moralist of duty thus posits a general obligation to keep promises.[20]

And Fried summarises:

> There exists a convention that defines the practice of promising and its entailments. This convention provides a way that a person may create expectations in others. By virtue of the basic Kantian principles of trust and respect, it is wrong to invoke that convention in order to make a promise, and then to break it.[21]

Let us assess this argument. If a person has actually given *moral* grounds for another to expect performance, then her obligation to perform should indeed be a rather straightforward inference thereof (and I have no objection to the Kantian reasoning Fried employs for the purpose of making this inference). But should it really matter whether this was done specifically through the invocation of an existing social practice, or done in any other way? The intentionality that Fried emphasises—the promisor's freedom to invite the promisee's confidence or not—may well have a significant role to play in explaining the moral status of those special grounds for expectation that a promise creates, or in justifying the obligation not to frustrate such expectation; but this condition may be met regardless: a person may intentionally and freely 'invoke the bonds of trust' (to use Fried's expression) without the help, or even in the absence of, a social practice or convention whose function it is to do so. Why should the normative implications of such an act be any different? Perhaps it could be said that in order for bonds of trust to be successfully invoked, there has to *be* trust in the first place. But for that, too, there need not exist any particular social practice: certain people may trust certain other people even in a society in which mutual trust is a rare commodity altogether, and in which promising is not generally practised or even recognised.

Fried's argument concerning the function of the practice of promising shows why it is valuable—why such a practice is, or would be, a good thing. Such an argument may be all that is needed in order to establish that people should, in principle, be able to promise, that is to intentionally undertake obligations to others through acts of communication. But it does not show that people should not be able to, nor that they cannot, do the same in the absence of such a general practice. If it is good that people can utilise trust in their relationships, and promises promote this good—perhaps, indeed as the device that gives trust its sharpest form—then the crucial point is that *to promise* is to invoke the bonds of trust (or, at any rate, to put these bonds into good use). It does not matter whether this is somehow mediated or helped by the existence of an established

[20] *Ibid* at 17 (emphasis omitted).
[21] *Ibid.*

practice. Of course, it *could* be so mediated or helped. The existence of a general practice of promising can make it easier to promise in much the same way that the availability of conventional linguistic means for promising can have that effect. (As an act of communication, promising would probably be simplest to perform where both obtain.) Moreover, where a well-established and largely accepted practice is in place, parties may be more likely to have, or may more readily acquire, a shared understanding of the normative implications of a promise, something which could boost further the efficiency with which promises fulfil at least some of their intended roles.[22] Yet, similarly to the case with the availability of conventional means, not the feasibility nor the binding force of a promise, at least inasmuch as it is perceived as a device whose function and value lie in facilitating bonds of trust, should be conditioned upon it being made as part or against the background of a general social practice of promising.[23]

The point could perhaps be reinforced if we try to isolate the 'social practice' element, or even the 'expectations-creating invocation of a social practice' element, from the qualities that such a practice may possess specifically on account of being a practice of promising, and which might be capable, as I have just suggested, of explaining the binding force of promises regardless of whether or not promising is in fact a practice. Take a practice such as greeting one's neighbour when sharing a ride in the lift. Let us suppose that such a practice is in place in the community to which I have recently relocated, and that I conform to it, freely, intentionally, the first time I share a ride with one of my neighbours. (To keep things simple, let us also assume that according to the practice in question it is I who have to say 'hello' first.) By this I surely give the neighbour grounds to expect a similar performance next time we meet in similar circumstances. But is it my obligation? What if, next time around, I am simply not in the mood, and fail to say 'hello': this could no doubt insult the neighbour. But would it amount to insulting him in that Kantian sense that Fried alludes to when explaining the obligation to keep a promise? Have I been *using* my neighbour, failing to respect or treat him as a person? Although I cannot here give Kant's Categorical Imperative due consideration, I suspect that to answer these questions in the positive would amount to giving a seriously exaggerated inter-

---

[22] That is likely to be the case, for instance, inasmuch as promises are expected to fulfil a co-ordinative function. Conversely, a largely accepted practice may make it harder to make (or achieve co-ordination through) promissory arrangements that, while morally acceptable (and thus, other things being equal, binding), differ in certain respects from the accepted practice.

[23] For a statement of a similar view see Raz, 'Promises and Obligations', above n 11, at 214–15. For a thorough discussion of the topic see TM Scanlon, 'Promises and Practices' (1990) 19 *Philosophy and Public Affairs* 199. Note that the argument according to which the binding force of a promise does not depend on the existence of a practice is not incompatible with an argument according to which the existence of a practice gives rise to an additional reason to think that promise-breaking is wrong, for instance as something which could undermine a valuable social practice, or, as in John Rawls' account, as a consequence of a principle of fairness (by making a promise the promisor 'accepts the benefits of a just arrangement'). See *A Theory of Justice* (Cambridge, Massachusetts, 1971) 344–48).

pretation to a moral outlook that may be suspected for being somewhat exaggerated regardless.

But maybe not: perhaps it could be argued that the only difference between promise-breaking and the failure to greet—the difference behind the intuition that keeping a promise is more important or serious, perhaps more obligatory, so to speak, than saying 'hello'—is one of degree, or of intensity: the insult inflicted by breaking a promise is simply greater than that inflicted by the failure to greet. Perhaps; yet I believe that to reduce the (morally significant) difference between the two types of behaviour to the terms of this equation is to miss a crucial aspect of the wrongness of promise-breaking, and to give a very incomplete account of the nature of promising. Despite the fact that in both cases legitimate expectations have been created through the intentional invocation of a social practice, the expectations created through promising can be shown to have a different status from that of the expectations created in the neighbour through conformity to the practice of greeting, and the requirement not to frustrate them can be shown to be linked to 'the basic Kantian principles of trust and respect,' in a way that the requirement to greet is not. And the difference cannot be explained away merely by pointing out (as Fried does) that promising is a practice *whose function it is* to create expectations, for that only begs the question. The difference must reflect something which is special to promises as a means of creating expectations, regardless of whether or not promising happens to be a social practice in a given community.

Having rejected the social practice thesis, what about the 'bootstrap quality' of the argument? Indeed, the problem in Fried's argument could be traced back to his understanding of this quality, or the problem to which it gives rise. The proposition that 'to have force in a particular case promises must be assumed to have force generally' is ambiguous, and it is correct only inasmuch as the assumption involved is understood as a normative matter, and not as a matter of social fact. For a particular promise to be considered binding there must be *reasons for thinking* that promises in general are binding; it must be assumed that promises in general *should* be held to be binding. And *this* proposition, to which we may or may not wish to refer as a bootstrap quality, reflects not something which 'lies behind every conventional structure'[24] (or, for that matter, every social practice), but rather is something which goes to the heart of normative reasoning in general. Far from paradoxical, it flows directly from a rather elementary principle of rational thought.

Yet Fried's argument, the above criticism notwithstanding, is far from worthless. Establishing that a general practice by which promises are held to be binding is, or would be, a good thing, is the most solid foundation on which to explain the binding force of promises; and much of his argument is precisely that: an explanation as to why the practice is a good thing. This explanation, moreover, does touch on what is indeed a key to the practice's main function

[24] *Contract as Promise*, at 12.

and value, namely the relationship between promise and trust. In the remainder of this chapter I will explore this relationship further.

Trust as a Condition

Trust, it has been stated, plays a crucial role in the practice of promising. In Fried's account, as we have seen, the notion that promising is an invocation of bonds of trust holds the key to the practice's main function and value, and, consequently, to the binding force of promises. But how exactly should this role be understood? Having rejected the emphasis placed by Fried on promising being a social practice (as part of the explanation of the binding force of promises), I suggested, in the previous section, that perhaps all that needs to obtain in order for bonds of trust to be invoked through promise-making is, simply, trust. But does that mean that pre-existing trust between parties is a condition for promising? And if so, in what sense? Is it impossible to promise where there is no trust to invoke? Is it futile?

One way of approaching such questions consists of examining the case of a promise that indeed fails to invoke bonds of trust. The precise implications of such a failure could be analysed with the help of JL Austin's classic account of the different things we do when performing a speech act. I will introduce briefly the pertinent vocabulary and distinctions, before returning to the case in hand.

Apart from the 'locutionary' act—roughly, the elements which together amount to producing meaningful units of speech—Austin distinguished between what he called the 'illocutionary' and 'perlocutionary' dimensions of a speech act, the illocution being the 'force' of the words (giving advice, asking, warning, thanking, etc), and the perlocution being the 'consequential effect' brought about by the words.[25] (When saying 'don't do that,' for example, the speaker may perform the illocutionary act of *ordering*, and the perlocutionary act of *stopping* the addressee from doing something.) All three types of act (or dimensions of a speech act), Austin emphasised, are subject to the possibility of failure in performance: 'We must systematically be prepared to distinguish,' he reminded us, 'between "the act of doing *x*", ie achieving *x*, and "the act of attempting to do *x*." '[26] A locutionary failure (which is of little interest for the purposes of our discussion) is characterised as a failure 'to get the words out, to express ourselves clearly, etc.'[27] The successful performance of an illocutionary act consists in 'bringing about the understanding of the meaning and of the force of the locution . . . the securing of *uptake*.'[28] Here we find two distinct types of

---

[25] See JL Austin, *How to Do Things with Words* (2nd edn, Oxford, 1975), especially Lectures 7–10.

[26] *Ibid* at 105.

[27] *Ibid* at 106. 'To express ourselves clearly' is notably ambiguous. What Austin apparently had in mind, as the context makes clear, is the basic failure to produce intelligible words or sentences.

[28] *Ibid* at 117.

potential failure. The failure to secure uptake of what Austin refers to narrowly as the 'meaning' of the words would occur, most obviously, when the addressee mishears the speaker (or, similarly, misreads handwriting, etc). A second type of illocutionary failure occurs, by contrast, where despite the fact that the words themselves were properly understood, their intended 'force' was not. Let us here take 'illocutionary failure' to denote exclusively the latter type of failure. It is exemplified by cases such as where the words 'thank you,' uttered with the intention of thanking, are understood by the addressee as an ironic expression of disapproval (eg for not helping enough), or where the words 'you can't do it,' meant as a statement of fact, as advice, or as a command, are understood as a dare. In all such cases, according to Austin's analysis, it would be true to say that the speaker merely tried, but failed, to thank, to advise, etc.[29] Finally, a perlocutionary failure occurs when an order, for instance, which was properly understood *as an order*, is disobeyed, advice (given in the hope that the addressee will follow or at least consider it) is disregarded, an invitation refused, and the like. By contrast to all other types of failure mentioned thus far, the perlocutionary failure, it may be said, is not in itself a failure in communication. In cases of perlocutionary failure alone (that is, following locutionary and illocutionary successes) the speaker succeeds in giving an order, inviting, advising, but merely fails to achieve the additional, 'consequential' effect that these acts of communication were intended to achieve (obedience to the order, acceptance of the invitation, heeding the advice).[30]

With these distinctions in place, how should the failure to invoke trust through promising be classified? The strongest form that the notion that trust is a necessary condition for promising could conceivably take, would be the thesis according to which the failure at stake amounts to an illocutionary failure—a failure *to promise*. Could such a thesis be defended?

'Trust' could, of course, mean different things in different contexts, and could be a matter of degree. For the purposes of the current exercise, however, let us try to make to do with an intuitive notion of what (lack of) trust amounts to as an inter-personal attitude in the current context, and let us concentrate on cases involving its complete, rather than partial, absence. As Fried put it, '[a] promise invokes trust *in my future actions*.'[31] With this in mind, take the following example. Shortly before Jerry is due to take his driving test, his uncle Leo tells him this: 'I promise to buy you a Ferrari as soon as you get your driving licence.' Aware as he is that Uncle Leo could not afford a second-hand Mini, however, Jerry does not take this seriously. The promise(?) does not create any expectations in him nor generate the slightest hope of getting the car. Now according to the thesis in question, Leo did not only fail to achieve the (supposedly) intended

---

[29] The same is true, according to Austin, of cases involving the other two types of failure mentioned earlier.

[30] Situations where a speech act brings about an unintended effect can also be described as perlocutionary failures (see above n 25, at 106). For present purposes I will ignore this possibility.

[31] *Contract as Promise*, at 11 (emphasis added).

perlocution of his promise: he merely tried, but failed, to make a promise in the first place. Being trusted (by the promisee), in other words, is a necessary condition—a 'competence condition,' if you like—for performing the illocutionary act of promising, in much the same way that being perceived as serious, or as capable of seriousness, is a competence condition for giving advice (and not just for having your advice heeded or followed). In its absence, the very 'uptake' of the speech act of promising cannot be secured.

If this sounds altogether far-fetched, consider the following two points. First, it could be suggested that the main normative implications of such a thesis are not really at odds with our relevant moral intuitions. The notion that Uncle Leo failed to promise surely means that he is not now (other things being equal) obliged to buy Jerry (who, let us assume, has now passed his test) the Ferrari. But that seems right. The main, if not the whole, point of a promise is to establish a certain bond with the promisee, and if breaking a promise is wrong, it must be wrong, first and foremost, as something which is done to the promisee. If Leo has failed to undertake an obligation towards Jerry, this need not entail that he is not culpable in any way. He could be criticised, for instance, for *attempting* to promise irresponsibly, or even for treating his nephew disrespectfully, or in an insulting manner. But if promising Jerry that he would do something that he clearly could not do was an insult, could Leo possibly insult him any further by, predictably, failing to perform? By such a failure he would not frustrate any expectations, for he created none; he would not abuse trust, for none was invested in him. Similarly, if Jerry were to rest his case for getting the Ferrari on the insult that a failure to keep the promise would amount to, he could be accused of hypocrisy: he never expected his uncle to keep that promise, and so may have been offended by the very fact that it had been made; surely he could not be more offended, or offended *again*, now that it is indeed broken? All this, so the argument goes, points in the direction of conceding that Leo has failed to place himself under an obligation towards Jerry in the first place, a notion which, in turn, goes nicely with the thesis according to which Leo's failure was of the illocutionary kind.

If the first point fastened on the notion that to promise is to undertake an obligation *to another person*, the second point fastens on to the fact that a promisor purports to undertake *an obligation*. Here it could be pointed out that the binding force of an obligation forms part of its very concept, or at least that *a grasp* of the binding nature of an obligation is part and parcel of an adequate grasp of its concept. Thus, the promisee's belief that the promisor will not act accordingly, that is, her belief that the promisor will renege, indicates that no intention to undertake (by that very act of communication) an obligation was in fact communicated to the promisee.[32] The promisor, in other words, has failed

---

[32] Unless, that is, the failure to discharge the obligation is expected to occur uniquely in and due to circumstances where non-performance would be justified. The argument in the text pertains to cases where this qualification does not apply.

to convey to or to satisfy the promisee that she is in possession of the very concept of (undertaking) an obligation, and this has to be, the argument goes, a straightforward failure to secure 'uptake' of the intended force of the locution, much in the same way that a speaker who is taken by her addressee not to be in possession of the very concept of marriage is bound to fail in securing uptake when attempting to propose.

It is time to expose the 'trust as a necessary condition' thesis for the exaggeration that it is. The deeper intuition that this thesis may be understood to echo is that the act of promising inexorably involves two elements—an undertaking of an obligation, and communication with the promisee—and that the two cannot be entirely disentangled, in the sense that since the undertaking is done through or by the very act of communication, it is bound to fail, at least to a certain extent, when communication fails. I believe this deeper intuition to be sound (which is why, on the basis of the thought that the thesis in question echoes it, I described it as an exaggeration rather than an outright misconception).[33] The 'trust as a necessary condition' thesis, however, does not follow from the deeper intuition, and should be rejected regardless.

To deprive that thesis of what intuitive appeal it may have by now acquired, let us start by adding a twist to the example around which it was introduced. Suppose that between his making (or attempting to make) the promise and Jerry's driving test, Uncle Leo is the sole winner of the jackpot in a roll-over lottery draw. Would it still be clear that he is not under an obligation to buy Jerry the Ferrari? Would Jerry's insistence that the promise be kept still appear so out of place? Or suppose, too, that Leo was aware of his initial failure to invoke Jerry's trust, and is now thinking: 'Here's an opportunity for me to rehabilitate my image, and prove that I am a man of my word—a man who keeps his promises'; should he be accused of conceptual confusion? The fact that these questions seem to warrant a negative answer indicates that the intuitive response outlined earlier (the first point) may be owed not to the fact that the promise created no expectations nor to the notion that the illocutionary success of a promise depends on the promisee's trust, but rather owed to the prevalent notion that, morally speaking, a person cannot be under an obligation to do what she cannot do. This being the case, the example with its new twist may still be problematic: if it is thought that Leo is bound by his promise, it needs to be explained how he can now be under an obligation that he could not undertake at the time at which he purported to undertake it. This problem, I think, has a solution (probably involving a distinction between different kinds of

---

[33] Two alternatives to the notion that success in undertaking an obligation through promising depends on the success of communication with the promisee can, in principle, be suggested. The outright rejection of that notion is the view that the binding force of a promise (or its normative implications in general) does not depend in any way on its success as an act of communication with the promisee. A less far-reaching alternative, albeit one that generates its own difficulties, allows for the possibility of a *partial* failure to promise, in the sense that, when an attempt to promise which would otherwise be successful is marred by a failure of communication with the promisee, the promisor may be bound *but not to the promisee* (or that the undertaking is binding as a vow).

impossibility, possibly involving the construal of the original promise as a conditional or a long-standing undertaking that comes into effect as soon as its performance becomes no longer impossible), but we need not ponder it here. The crucial point is that the deciding factor is not Jerry's trust. The last problem could in fact be averted if we assume that Uncle Leo (though, still, not Jerry) had learnt about the lottery win before he made the promise. We could even assume that he made the promise anticipating that Jerry will not trust him to keep it, and specifically intending to prove him wrong. Should he in such a case be accused of an outright conceptual confusion? Again, a positive answer seems far from intuitive.

That still leaves us with the second point that was made in support of the 'trust as a necessary condition' thesis. If the binding force of an obligation is part of its very concept, how can Jerry's belief that Uncle Leo will not perform be reconciled with the notion that the latter secured uptake of his communicated intention to undertake an obligation? The answer is simple. As promises typically involve futurity, trusting a person to keep her promise typically involves matters over and above beliefs pertaining to the promisor's state of mind at the time of promising. The promisee may believe that the promisor fully grasps the concept of an obligation, and that at the time of promising she genuinely intends to undertake one (rather than, for instance, that she is merely *pretending* to have such an intention[34])—which, other things being equal, is all that is necessary for promising, as an act of communication with the promisee, to be complete[35]— and yet also believe that the promisor is certain to end up breaking the promise due to forgetfulness, for instance, or weakness of will, or due to circumstances of which she is not aware at the time but which will make performance impos-

---

[34] Should a 'lying promise'—a case where a person says she promises but does not genuinely intend to bind herself and perform—be considered a promise? The main reason to think that the answer is no, is that a promise is a voluntary undertaking of an obligation, whereas the lying promisor does not really intend to undertake, but is merely pretending to have such an intention. On this view it is still possible to hold the lying promisor bound by her 'promise,' but not by implication of the promise principle but as a case of estoppel, a principle that could be justified on the grounds of protecting the promisee, or protecting the practice of promising, against the harms caused through a fraudulent invocation of the practice. A similar principle can be relied upon in order to establish the (possibly limited) liability of a negligent promisor, a person who unwittingly acts in a way that makes it appear to be the case that she promised. (See Raz, 'Promises and Obligations', above n 11, at 214, n 5.) What about a case where a promise (?) that was made sincerely is mistaken by the promisee to be a lying promise? On the view that lying promises are not promises, this would probably have to be classified as a full-blown failure 'to secure uptake,' the implication being that the promise is not binding. I am not sure I am comfortable with this outcome, but the problem is of little significance for the purposes of the current discussion. A possible solution may be along the lines of the second alternative outlined above n 33.

[35] An attempt to promise may of course fail for reasons which have nothing to do with communicating successfully with the promisee, eg when promising to perform an intrinsically immoral act. A similar problem to that raised above n 34 in connection with 'lying promises' can arise in this context, too: what happens when the promisee believes that the obligation at stake cannot be undertaken because it is immoral, whereas in fact it is not? The difference, however, is that here there is no failure of communication (the promisee's mistake has to do with the *actual* force of the words, but not with their *intended* force) and so little reason to doubt the success of the undertaking.

sible. If, to return to our example, Jerry's case is like that—if he does not doubt Leo's sincerity or conceptual grasp, but, let us say, merely assumes that he is conspicuously ignorant of Ferrari prices or of his own financial ability—then the problem is not one of uptake, and his mistrust need not indicate nor amount to a failure by Leo to perform the illocutionary act of promising.

Before we close the lid on the 'trust as a necessary condition' thesis, I wish to look briefly at the more moderate form that such a thesis might take. The thesis examined thus far construed the promisor's failure to invoke, through promising, the promisee's trust as an illocutionary failure to promise. The more moderate thesis construes it as a *per*locutionary failure, that is, it is a thesis according to which promising where there is no trust, while not impossible, is bound to be futile. For such a thesis to be correct, it needs to be the case that the perlocutionary effect(s) that trust facilitates could not be achieved without trust, and that promising could not be used as a means of achieving other perlocutionary effects which do not depend on trust in the same way.

Neither, however, is true. As an earlier example illustrated, promising may be used in order to achieve at least one perlocutionary effect—proving a mistrusting promisee wrong—that not only does not depend on trust, but which makes sense particularly when trust is altogether absent or is at least in doubt. Furthermore, the perlocutionary effect which trust does usually facilitate can in fact be achieved without it. This possibility has been obscured in the discussion thus far by the fact that trust has been identified with its most conspicuous effect in the context, namely the promisee's confidence that the promise will be kept. Yet it is possible for such confidence to obtain even in circumstances where the promisee could not be said to trust the promisor in any credible sense of the word. Think, for instance, of a case where the promisee believes that, if left to her own devices, the promisor would certainly renege, and for no good reason— that she would simply forget about the promise, for instance—but that the promisor's mother, who is aware of the promise, will somehow make her keep it. It might be said here that the promisee trusts *that the promise will be kept*, but then 'trusts' is used in a different sense, very close to simply 'believes,' which does not at all pertain to the promisee's attitude towards the promisor. To insist that the promisee in this last scenario *trusts the promisor* would be to stretch the term far beyond its ordinary connotation.

The last point gives us a broad clue as to the sense in which 'trust' usually features in the framework of promising. Trusting a promisor may indeed mean, in practical terms, believing that (other things being equal) she will keep the promise; but it is a belief that reflects and flows from a certain favourable perception of the promisor's personality in general or, at least, relevant personal attributes, and that as such has to do not only with the likelihood that she will act in a certain way, but also with the reasons for which she is thought likely to do so— reasons which, in one sense or another, must be perceived as the right ones.[36]

---

[36] This point will be resumed and some pertinent distinctions will be introduced in chs 2 and 3.

Returning to our current concern, it can be concluded that the thesis according to which trust is a necessary condition for promising, either in the illocutionary or in the perlocutionary sense, fails. Yet while this thesis (or theses) goes too far, it goes too far in the right direction. It could be pointed out, tellingly, that the examples used in rebutting both of its versions centred on rather unusual circumstances—circumstances which could perhaps be said to epitomise the margins of the practice, but not its core. In the same vein it could be argued that trust, while not a necessary condition, is a *normal* condition for promising. Promises, that is, are normally made where there is trust, and it is normally in such an environment that they have the effect that, in terms of the interaction between promisor and promisee, they are most commonly intended to have. With its correlative, respect, trust holds the key to the practice's most significant values, instrumental and intrinsic, and to the main explanation as to why breaking a promise is wrong. By way of addressing a number of issues arising in and around the practice of promising, I now wish to illustrate and, in the process, further establish these claims.

Why Promise?

A promise is usually intended to generate confidence in the promisee with regard to, or facilitate reliance on, the promisor's future actions. For a promise to achieve this effect, the promisee usually has to trust the promisor. In rejecting the view that trust is a necessary condition for the successful performance of the perlocutionary act of promising, it was pointed out that promises are not always made in order to achieve such an effect (or, in other words, that there is no *one* perlocutionary act of promising). But cases where a promise is not intended to create confidence, and where its effectiveness does not hinge the way it usually does on the existence of trust, are not only less common; logically speaking, too, such cases are largely derivative or secondary to the normal use of the practice on the presumption of trust.

Take the case we have encountered earlier, of making a promise while knowing that it will create no expectations in a mistrusting promisee, with the intention of rehabilitating the promisor's reputation (in the eyes of the promisee, and possibly others) through subsequently keeping the promise. It is precisely as a device which is normally used in order to invoke trust, that a promise can serve as a means to that end. Indeed by keeping the promise, such a promisor can rehabilitate her reputation *as a trustworthy person*; she may have known that the promise will not create confidence, but by keeping it she intends to prove the promisee wrong on precisely that count. Or take another example of a promise which is not intended to achieve the normal perlocutionary effect: having received a negligible donation (say, 5p to make a phone call), a person promises to pay the donor back. As the latter is expected to wave the debt there and then, such a promise can be said to be intended as no more than a gesture of politeness or gratitude. But a promise can only fulfil this function on the presumption that, were the promisee to accept the promise, it would serve as a special reason for the promisor to pay back. In the absence of the kind of trust which supports this presumption, making the promise would be but an empty gesture.

Here we might be reminded of another point which was made in the context of rejecting the 'trust as a necessary condition' thesis: that a promise may some-times prove effective in creating confidence or facilitating reliance regardless of trust. But such cases, too, could be distinguished—and distinguished not only on the basis of their relative rarity—from those which deserve to be considered as illustrations of the normal function of the practice. They typically hinge on a number of contingencies over and above the promise itself, and over and above the relationship between promisor and promisee. For it to be thought likely that the promisor will, for instance, respond to some form of external pressure to keep the promise, it needs to be assumed that the fact of the promise will be known to others, that others are likely to react adversely in case of a breach, that such a reaction or the prospect of facing it would be a reason—reason enough—for the promisor to keep the promise, and so on. Moreover, the prospect of such pressure forming would normally depend in the first place on the acceptance, in the relevant quarters, of the notion that promises ought to be kept. And as we shall see, the strongest reasons to accept this notion derive from the desirability of promises as an effective device for invoking trust.

Why Want a Promise?

In analysing the normal function of a promise and the conditions under which it is normally fulfilled, it should be useful to note that promises are often made, rather than out of the blue or as a strictly gratuitous gesture, in situations where they are either explicitly or implicitly called for. And an examination of the rea-sons for which people may want to obtain a promise can serve to reinforce the observations of the previous section. What people usually hope to gain by obtaining a promise is reassurance regarding certain future actions of the prospective promisor. Thomas Scanlon correctly observed that 'when I say "I promise to be there at ten o'clock to help you," the effect is the same as if I had said "I will be there at ten o'clock to help you. Trust me." '[37] By the same token it can be said that when I tell someone that I will be there to help her and she replies by saying 'Can you promise me that you will?' (or simply: 'Promise?'), the effect is the same as if she had asked 'Can I trust you on that?,' or 'Can I rely on your help?'

An equivalent point to that which was made in the previous section could be made here concerning the relationship between, on the one hand, the normal reason for wanting a promise and the normal conditions—namely trust—under

[37] Above n 23, at 211.

which obtaining a promise would (in terms of that reason) be effective, and, on the other hand, cases where the practice is employed effectively but for a different purpose, or under different conditions. Such cases are bound to be not only less usual, but logically derivative as well. Thus, to borrow an example from Joseph Raz, a person may 'solicit a promise, hoping and believing that it will be broken, in order to prove to a certain lady how unreliable the promisor is.'[38] Here the point that the promisee is trying to prove and for which he solicits the promise is specifically about the promisor, not about promising in general; and the point, clearly unfavourable, is meant to be proved by demonstrating that a promise obtained from that person should not be taken to provide that with which a promise is *normally* expected to provide the promisee. Or take a person who wishes to lend some financial support to a friend in need, believing yet not minding that he will not be able to pay back. Suspecting, however, that the friend is too proud or would be embarrassed to accept an outright donation, she offers to give him the money only if he promises to pay it back. Here, too, the promisee is not hoping to gain reassurance or encouragement to rely, and does not trust (in the relevant sense) the promisor. Yet it is precisely because promises are normally asked for in order to gain reassurance and on the presumption of trust that the promisee's ploy may succeed, with the promisor getting the impression that the money is given as a loan, in the hope and belief that it will be repaid.

What is Wrong with Breaking a Promise?

There may be more than one reason for thinking that breaking a promise is wrong. Earlier it has been suggested that since the main point of promising is to establish a certain bond with another person, if breaking a promise is wrong then it is wrong, first and foremost (though by no means exclusively), as something which is done to or in connection with the promisee. It is this aspect of promise-breaking that I wish to comment on in this section. In doing so, I will follow the philosophical trend of drawing an analogy between promise-breaking and lying.[39]

Behind such analogies is the notion that lying and promise-breaking amount to harming or mistreating a person (the person lied to, the promisee) in a similar sense, so that the wrongness of both could be explained along similar lines, or the requirement to refrain from either could be shown to derive from one,

---

[38] 'Promises and Obligations,' above n 11, at 213.

[39] A notable example is Warnock's analysis of the promissory obligation as derived from the general moral requirement of veracity (see Warnock, above n 7). For a powerful critique of Warnock's argument see Don Locke's 'The Object of Morality, and the Obligation to Keep a Promise' (1972) 2 *Canadian Journal of Philosophy* 135. The thrust of my own argument concerning the alleged analogy is largely in line with, and was partly influenced by, Locke's argument. See also *Contract as Promise*, at 16–17.

more general moral requirement. The apparent similarity between the two cases, to be more specific, has to do with the notion that the liar and the promise-breaker both deceive the addressee. Whereas the liar attempts to deceive by the very act of communication she performs, the promise-breaker first attempts, by promising, to make the promisee adopt a certain belief, and then, by breaking the promise, allows this belief to become false.[40] Now I have no objection to the construal, along such lines, of promise-breaking as deception. But as such, given the particular nature of the beliefs which promises are normally intended to create and the particular method of creating beliefs that promising is, I consider it to be a special case of deception—special, as I will now argue, in a sense that likening promise-breaking to lying can only serve to obscure or understate.

Let us start by looking at lying. A particularly strong argument to the effect that lying is wrong shows it to be subversive of rationality or personal autonomy. The structure of such an argument may look roughly like this. The rational agent strives to judge, plan, choose, on the basis of true information. The autonomous person seeks to exercise a measure of control over her life, fashioning it through freely-made decisions and choices. Being in possession of true information is a basic requirement in order for people to put their rational capacity into good effect, and in order for them to lead successful autonomous lives. To lie is to try to make people adopt false beliefs. It thus stands in sharp contrast to the notion of treating people with the kind of respect they warrant as rational agents, or as agents whose legitimate endeavour it is to enjoy personal autonomy.[41]

Such an argument can, I believe, explain the harmful effect—and the wrongness—of certain lies; but as a general explanation for why lying is wrong, or as a justification of a general duty to refrain from lying, it fails. For there is nothing in the concept or the practice of lying to suggest that lies are always, or even normally, told with regard to matters which are of any relevance to the hearer's life, or told with the intention or the effect of concealing information which could in any way affect or serve as a basis for her plans, decisions, or choices, or, more generally, told with regard to matters which the hearer can reasonably be said to have an interest (or, at any rate, a legitimate interest) in knowing the truth about simply on account of possessing a capacity for rationality or autonomy. Indeed lies are often told with regard to matters which are none of these things; and if telling such lies is wrong, it must be wrong for a different, probably less powerful, reason. It is safe to say, in any event, that as far as the general concept of lying can indicate and as the variety of common circumstances and motives for lying confirms, the relevance or the significance of the information contained in a lie

---

[40] This characterisation is based mainly on Warnock's argument. See *ibid.*

[41] A particularly thorough modern attempt to argue along such lines is Fried's, in *Right and Wrong* (Cambridge, Massachusetts, 1978) ch 3. For a pertinent argument concerning the relationship between information and judgment, between judgment and rationality, and between rationality and truth, see also HI Brown, *Rationality* (London and New York, 1988) chs 4, 5.2, 5.3.

(or, similarly, the relevance or significance of the information that a lie is designed to conceal) for the person or people to whom it is told is a mere contingency.

Is it any different with promises? We have already encountered cases where a promisee has no real interest in the promise being kept, and where a promise is given in the knowledge that its subject matter is of negligible significance for the promisee. But in examining such cases we have also seen that they are not characteristic of the practice. Promises are normally solicited, and given, when special reassurance concerning the promisor's future actions is required. And such reassurance is normally required, we may now add, with regard to matters which are of some significance for the promisee. Focusing on the futurity that promises usually involve, it can be surmised that a promise is typically significant for the promisee precisely as a guarantor of some future event that impinges on her plans, and that, as such, substantially informs her decisions or choices. The non-occurrence of that event—the breaking of the promise—is thus particularly likely to be harmful in ways which lies only contingently are.

Several writers on promises have contended that the promisee must necessarily benefit from, or have an interest in, the performance of the promise, or that upon promising the promisor must believe this to be the case.[42] This view has come under forceful attack, notably by Raz, one of whose counter-examples—the promisee who wished to prove the promisor's unreliability—I borrowed earlier.[43] A distinction which has been overlooked in this context, however, is that between having an interest in (or benefiting from) the subject matter of a promise, and having an interest in obtaining the promise itself. The separability of the two, not only as a conceptual matter but also as a practical proposition, was in fact illustrated clearly in that very example, as well as in the other example I introduced alongside it (soliciting a promise in order to make the promisor comfortable about accepting financial support): in both cases the promisee is positively interested in obtaining a promise to do something in which he or she has no real interest.[44] This distinction makes room for a thesis occupying the middle ground between the view that promises can only be given to do things that would benefit the promisee or that the promisee desires (or only inasmuch

---

[42] See eg J Searle, *Speech Acts* (Cambridge, 1969) ch 3, and, for a more cautious reiteration of this view, Warnock, above n 7, at 111–12. ('I suppose that the person or persons to whom a promise is made will be those who have an interest in the doing of the thing promised . . . I could not, perhaps scarcely could, promise you that I will give up smoking, if you do not care a straw whether I give up smoking or not.')

[43] Above n 38 and text. See also WR Carter, 'On Promising the Unwanted' (1972/3) 33 *Analysis* 88.

[44] In these cases the promisees can also be said to be interested in obtaining a promise, but not in its performance (indeed, in Raz's example the promisee is positively hoping for non-performance). Note, however, that the possibility of having an interest in a promise but not in its subject matter need not always coincide with such an attitude: it is possible to imagine a situation where a person who is interested in obtaining (or, at any rate, is willing to obtain) a promise while having no interest in its subject matter, would still wish it to be kept, for instance as a sign of respect by the promisor, or out of concern for the latter's reputation.

as the promisor so believes), and the view according to which anything can, in principle, be promised to anybody, wholly regardless of the promisee's attitude. While eschewing the notion that the promisee must have an interest in the subject matter of the promise, such a thesis holds the promisee's interest in, or at least willingness to accept, the promise itself, or the promisor's belief that the promisee is so interested or willing, to be a necessary condition for promising.

One thing which to my mind makes such a thesis attractive is its implications in terms of the significance attached to the promisee's attitude toward the promise, and the kind of leverage that goes with that. For it is hardly controversial that the promisee has the power to release the promisor from her obligation. But then this power can also be a responsibility, and it seems strange that a (would-be) promisee should not be able to avoid assuming it in the first place, or that a person should be able to thrust such a responsibility upon another, regardless of whether or not the latter is at all interested in finding herself in this position, and regardless of whether or not the promisor even believes this to be the case. In terms of its intuitive appeal, moreover, it is worth noting that the thesis in question is compatible with both of the counter-examples Raz provided when refuting the view that the promisee must be interested in the promise's subject matter. In one, as we saw, the promisee actively solicits the promise and has a clear interest in obtaining it. In the other—a youth promises his father, who protests that he sees nothing wrong in smoking, never to smoke—it is said that the latter 'reluctantly accepts' the promise.[45] Now Raz was of course correct in concluding that the youth's belief that he had promised should not warrant an accusation of conceptual confusion. But would this still be the case without the acceptance, albeit reluctant, of the promise by the promisee? To make sure that our reaction to this scenario is not confused by the father's glaring ignorance about the hazards of smoking, let us assume that he is not ignorant, and that his son tries to promise him that he will take up smoking in due course. Should we now accuse the youth of conceptual confusion? I tend to think that we should, rather than so accuse his father if he replies: 'You *cannot* promise me this—I'm not interested!'

I will not, however, undertake to defend this thesis any further here. Our current interest lies, after all, in the normal, not the necessary, circumstances and conditions for promising. And in light of what has been established thus far with regard to these, it can safely be said that typically, the promisee is interested *both* in obtaining the promise itself and in its subject matter, with her interest in the former largely being a reflection of the strength of her interest in the latter.

So what is wrong with promise-breaking? The discussion thus far, highlighting the special interest the promisee normally has in the performance of a promise and, accordingly, the particular harm she is likely to sustain when her

---

[45] 'Promises and Obligations,' above n 11, at 214. Note that this example is different from those which were discussed previously in that here the promisor is aware of the promisee's lack of interest in the subject matter of the promise.

belief that it will be performed proves to be false, brings us close to finding a powerful answer. But we are not quite there yet. When a lie has the similar harmful effect of making a person adopt some false belief so that her decisions or choices (decisions or choices which, we must assume, she is entitled to make) stand on shaky ground, her (legitimate) plans are thwarted, the step required on the way to establishing the wrong of telling that lie is fairly straightforward. Lies are typically told, after all, with the specific intention to deceive. But, 'lying promises' aside,[46] it is different with promise-breaking. At the time of making the promise, the promisor may have no intention of deceiving the promisee in any way—she may well intend to keep it. And at the time of breaking the promise, she need not have an intention to deceive either—she may have forgotten about the promise, or simply changed her mind. What is wrong with that?

Again, we come to the subject of trust. If a promise is to be construed as an attempt to make the promisee adopt a certain belief, then it can be said that for this attempt to succeed, the promisor needs to obtain something from the promisee, something that only the promisee can provide her with: his trust. To promise is to invoke trust, and for a promise to be effective this trust (normally) needs to be given. The promisee's trust, if you like, is what the promisor needs in order to gain access to and plant a belief in the promisee's mind. Now other things being equal, asking for, and using, something which is the promisee's in order to gain access to and plant a belief in his mind, can only be considered a legitimate enterprise so long as it is done in a manner which is at least compatible with his interests. Using the promisee's trust, having intentionally invoked it, in a way which is not compatible with his interests, let alone in a way which amounts to positively harming him, would be a clear cut and a rather extreme case of taking advantage, of using a person. Promise-breaking, we have seen, is likely to have a particularly harmful effect on the promisee; respect for the promisee's interests normally entails keeping the promise. Accordingly, promising is legitimate, other things being equal, only as long as the promisor assumes, and discharges, a special responsibility towards the promisee: the responsibility to prevent the belief he has been invited or made to adopt from proving or becoming false, or, simply, the responsibility to keep the promise. An unjustified failure to discharge this responsibility, we can now appreciate, is indeed a blatant and rather paradigmatic violation of, in Fried's words, 'the basic Kantian principles of trust and respect.'

It could be suggested that, as far as the role played by trust in the last argument is concerned, the same is true of lying, for the use of language in general (or, at any rate, when producing affirmatives) entails a tacit invocation of the addressee's trust. Writing about lying, Fried, for instance, has argued along these lines: 'Every lie necessarily implies—as does every assertion—an assurance, a warranty of its truth,' so that '[e]very lie is a broken promise.'[47] And yet

---

[46] See above n 34.
[47] Above n 41, at 67.

I would insist that the case of promise-breaking—if only, in this respect, as a matter of degree—still is distinct. The difference is perhaps akin to that between an implied warranty, and the warranty which is boldly advertised in order to lure the customer into the deal in the first place: both should be respected, but we may feel that a failure to respect the latter is somehow 'more wrong,' more offensive, or more exploitative than a failure to respect the former.

The Value of Promise

The discussion of the previous section makes sense, and its conclusions stand, only if it is assumed that promising (the practice by which people voluntarily undertake obligations to others) is valuable. If it were not, there would be little reason to think that it should generally succeed in fulfilling the function or functions it is normally intended to fulfil, little reason to think that its basic rules should be adhered to. In this section I wish to take a closer look at this assumption.

I have described the normal reasons to make and to obtain a promise, as well as, correspondingly, the conditions under which promises are normally made, in terms and in light of the role trust plays in the practice. The wrong of promise-breaking and the (normal) justification for the obligation to keep a promise were then analysed in a similar vein. Thus it should come as no surprise that trust holds the key to the quandary which, in a sense, underlies all of these previous discussions; that is, the practice is valuable precisely because a promise is, to re-invoke Fried's eloquent formulation, '[t]he device that gives trust its sharpest, most palpable form.'[48]

Promise is valuable as a practice capable of fulfilling two distinct functions, both related to the particular use it makes, in its normal mode of operation, of trust. What I shall refer to as the *instrumental* value of the practice is the focus of Fried's own account of the purpose of promising:

> In order that I be as free as possible, that my will have the greatest possible range consistent with the similar will of others, it is necessary that there be a way in which I may commit myself. It is necessary that I be able to make nonoptional a course of conduct that would otherwise be optional for me. By doing this I can facilitate the projects of others, because I can make it possible for those others to count on my future conduct, and thus those others can pursue more intricate, more far-reaching projects.[49]

And, fixing specifically on the 'more central' situation where a reciprocal gain is sought, Fried schematises the function of the practice as follows:

---

[48] *Contract as Promise*, at 8
[49] *Ibid* at 13.

You want to accomplish purpose A and I want to accomplish purpose B. Neither of us can succeed without the cooperation of the other. Thus I want to be able to commit myself to help you achieve A so that you will commit yourself to help me achieve B.[50]

In the particular context of Fried's account of this often commented-upon function of the practice, it may be felt that the 'instrumental' label sells the argument short. For as the first of these two quotes attests, Fried sensibly depicts the co-operation- or reliance-facilitating function of the practice as a constitutive element of personal freedom. Yet this function and value could be distinguished from a much less often commented-upon good that promising promotes—a feature to which I shall exclusively refer as the *intrinsic* value of the practice. This time, let us take our cue from Raz. The principles stating when promises are binding, he wrote:

> present promises as creating a relation between the promisor and the promisee—which is taken out of the general competition of conflicting reasons. It creates a special bond, binding the promisor to be, in the matter of the promise, partial to the promisee. It obliges the promisor to regard the claim of the promisee as not just one of the many claims that every person has for his respect and help but as having peremptory force. Hence [the principles stating when promises are binding] can only be justified if the creation of such special relationships between people is held to be valuable.[51]

In his discussion of the issue, Raz did not elaborate on the value or the desirability of those 'special relationships.' It could of course be suggested that they are desirable precisely because they enable their parties to achieve the kind of co-operation or mutual reliance in which the instrumental value of the practice lies, in which case the argument does not differ substantially from that of Fried. But the link which Raz highlights between promising and relationships hints at another proposition. Special relationships between people, relationships the parties to which are united by bonds that do not exist between people in general, can be said to be valuable in themselves, regardless of the possibility of co-operation or the co-ordinated pursuit of various projects which are essentially external to the relationship. If so, then promising, not only as a practice by which people undertake obligations to others, but particularly as a practice grounded, as it is, in trust and respect, may be valuable—intrinsically valuable—for its capacity to promote and reinforce personal relationships.

It should be easy to appreciate that the very possibility of individually-owed obligations can be conducive to relationships, and voluntarily-undertaken (individually-owed) obligations in particular. But there is a more intriguing way in which to understand the contribution of promises to relationships, related specifically to the potential role of promises as manifestations of trust and respect. Inasmuch as it is possible to generalise in this context, it can be said that

---

[50] *Contract as Promise*, at 13.
[51] 'Promises and Obligations,' above n 11, at 227–28.

trust and respect are among the most fundamental building blocks of personal relationships. Both, however, are a kind of attitude; and an attitude that does not find its manifestation is, in a sense, a mere potential. Promising is a unique device with which to realise this potential. To promise is to invoke trust; on the promisee's part, to take the promise seriously, as intended, is (normally) to give that trust, to show that it exists; and to keep the promise is to justify the promisee's trust, to prove trustworthy, to show respect. Promises are intrinsically valuable, if you like, as an exercise in the deployment of trust and respect in the framework of the relationship between promisor and promisee. As such they may be valuable regardless of the value attached to that form of co-operation (or co-ordination, or reliance) they facilitate, and over and above the value, if any, of those projects the pursuit of which co-operation makes possible.[52]

In terms of the significance of trust for the realisation of each of the practice's two primary functions, there is an important difference between the instrumental and the intrinsic value of promising. We have seen that promises are normally effective in fulfilling their instrumental function when made under conditions of trust. But we have seen also that the kind of confidence that a promise is usually meant to create in the promisee—the confidence upon which its instrumental usefulness hinges—can sometimes be achieved without trust, just as a promisor may sometimes have powerful reasons or motives to keep the promise which bear little on her trustworthiness. By contrast, promising can only fulfil its intrinsic function as a practice through which trust and respect find systematic expression when these attitudes are in fact, or at least are believed to be, behind the participants' actions and reactions. For alternative motives (to keep a promise) and sources of reassurance (that a promise will be kept) of the kind that can support the practice's instrumental function and in this respect replace or lessen the significance of trust, would tend, if anything, to undermine the practice's function as enhancer of relationships. Not only is it the case that the known existence of such motives and sources can sometimes blur those messages of trust and respect that partaking in the practice can otherwise serve to convey, but their intentional or explicit invocation in the framework of a relationship can in fact positively damage, rather than reinforce, the relationship: it can be taken as evidence that trust, perhaps the kind of inter-personal trust which the parties expect to enjoy, does not in fact obtain.

Promises between Strangers

The potential contribution of promises to personal relationships will be explored in some greater detail at a later stage. The issue is of particular significance, as I

---

[52] Focusing on trust, John Finnis expressed a similar thought in his discussion of promising: 'Mutual trustworthiness is not merely a means to further distinct ends; it is in itself a valuable component of any common life': JM Finnis, *Natural Law and Natural Rights* (Oxford, 1980) 306.

will argue, for the purposes of comparing promises to their legal equivalents, contracts. Before we move on, however, I wish to comment briefly on a related issue which is similarly pertinent to that comparison.

Although not much has been said thus far with regard to the kind of trust promises (normally) involve and derive much of their value from, enough has been said to suggest that it is a kind of trust which cannot generally be expected to obtain between people. Rather, it is the kind of trust which is likely to be the product of some previous acquaintance with a person, or based on some more or less informed impression of her personality. Indeed, promises are normally made in the framework of on-going relationships[53]—a fact which bears weightily not only on the nature of this practice but particularly, and in a much overlooked way, on the analogy between promises and contracts, the latter being agreements typically made outside the context of an already-existing relationship, in a framework designed primarily to enable just that.

Yet promises are sometimes made, and made effectively, between strangers. That in itself should not be too puzzling, as trust has been described merely as a normal, not a necessary condition. But promises are sometimes made between strangers in order to achieve what promises are normally meant, in the instrumental sense, to achieve; and such promises sometimes prove effective regardless of the presence of any of those special elements—such as the distinct possibility that breaking the promise would have a detrimental effect on the promisor—which sometimes render promises (instrumentally) effective despite the absence of the element which normally plays this role, namely trust. Does this call my account of promising into question?

I do not think that it does, for the possibility of promises between strangers is not only an exception, but an exception which largely reflects the logic of what has been described as the rule; that is, such promises can be understood to derive their force (not necessarily their normative force, but their practical force, their efficacy) from the normal operation of the practice in the framework of ongoing relationships, under the conditions of pre-existing trust. Here is why.

When I make a promise to a stranger, I tell her something about myself. I invoke a practice which is normally used in the framework of established relationships and which is grounded in trust and respect, by this implying that I am the kind of person who plays by this practice's rules—that I am, in the relevant sense, trustworthy, that I treat people, *and will treat her*, with respect. The promisee may or may not believe that this is indeed the case; and if she does not, the promise would likely prove ineffective, and fail to create the intended confidence in the promisee.[54] But then if the promisee does take my promise as a reason to believe that I will do what I promised to do, if the promise—which, let us assume, was made sincerely—proves effective, then in a very limited yet sig-

---

[53] See Raz, above n 13, at 932, 934.

[54] For simplicity's sake, I am ignoring for the moment the fact that confidence, trust, strength of belief and the like can all be a matter of degree.

nificant sense we are no longer complete strangers. By the very act of putting the practice of promising into use—I by making the promise, inviting trust, suggesting respect; the promisee by taking the promise as a source of confidence, by trusting—we emulate the behaviour of people in a relationship. The keeping of the promise then closes a circle through which we establish a bond of trust and respect, thus somewhat removing ourselves, so to speak, from the domain of strangerhood. Stated plainly, the point is that the practicality of promises between strangers hinges on the actors' very disposition to treat each other, for the matter of the promise and as far as the promise is concerned, the way people do not normally, or at least cannot generally be expected to, treat strangers. If you like, effective promises between complete strangers are possible, but the more effective, the more likely a promise is to render its parties no longer complete strangers.

2

Normativity, Trust, and Threats

T HE PREVIOUS CHAPTER examined the practice of promising, focusing in
particular on the role of trust in the practice. I argued that promises are
normally made under conditions of trust, that the normal functioning of the
practice under such conditions renders it intrinsically valuable, and that trust
plays a crucial role in the (normal) justification of the duty to keep a promise. I
also implied that things may be different when it comes to contracts. My main
argument concerning the differences between contract and promise, partly in
terms of the role and the significance of trust in each of these practices, will be
introduced in the next chapter. In this chapter I wish to take a detour which will
hopefully pave the way for that later discussion. I will examine a thesis launched
primarily as a critique of HLA Hart's analysis of the way in which the law, criminal law in particular, purports to guide behaviour.

The thesis in question warrants our attention despite the disparity in terms of
subject matter. It suggests that the law's use of coercion to secure compliance
with its directives excludes trust and respect, and leaves no scope for normativity. The role designated for coercion is particularly conspicuous, perhaps, in
criminal law. But coercion, or at any rate the coercive potential of the law, plays
an important role in the context of private law, too. Thus if successful, this thesis could have a devastating effect on the alleged analogy between promissory
and contractual relations, between contract and promise—devastating in particular in light of the suggested analysis of the latter in Chapter 1.

I hope I am not giving too much of the game away by saying that, in the first
part of this chapter, I intend to reject much of the thrust of the thesis in question. As the arguments provided in its support touch on a number of issues
which themselves are of significance for the study of the relationship between
contract and promise, its examination should prove conducive to this study nevertheless.

I. THE DISJUNCTIVE VIEW

Following HLA Hart, we can distinguish between two methods of guiding behaviour which the law may be said to employ. On the one hand, there is the use of
threats: providing people with a reason for conformity by attaching sanctions to

non-compliance.[1] On the other hand, there is the method we may refer to as the 'normative' (or simply 'normativity'). Hart described the latter as the 'characteristic technique' and the 'primary purpose' of criminal law:

> There are many techniques by which society may be controlled, but the characteristic technique of the criminal law is to designate by rules certain types of behaviour as standards for the guidance either of the members of society as a whole or of special classes within it: they are expected without the aid or intervention of officials to understand the rules and to see that the rules apply to them and to conform to them.[2]

By contrast, the punitive aspect of the law is explained as merely supportive and secondary to the normative method:

> Only when the law is broken, and this primary function of the law fails, are officials concerned to identify the fact of breach and impose the threatened sanctions.[3]

We can see that in Hart's view, the idea of the two 'techniques' being employed together is perfectly viable, with sanctions operating as a kind of 'fallback' option, reserved for and utilised in cases where the normative method fails to fulfil its function of securing conformity with the law.[4] This view was recently challenged, in quite an ingenious way, by Meir Dan-Cohen.[5] Dan-Cohen's main thesis, as the name he gives it, 'the disjunctive view,' suggests, calls into question the very notion that threats and normativity can dwell together, let alone the notion that the 'coercive' aspect of the law is secondary to the normative. The basic idea is this:

> [S]anctions cannot be simply appended to antecedently and independently existing norms without affecting them. Rather than being just complementary and mutually reinforcing devices, normativity and coercion are also at odds with each other.[6]

And, aimed specifically at Hart's view of the matter:

> 'A request backed by a sanction' is an oxymoron. The case of authority . . . is similar. 'A norm backed by a sanction' presents an incongruity that the prevailing additive conception of authority ignores.[7]

Dan-Cohen starts his defence of the disjunctive view with an attempt to endow it with intuitive appeal. Drawing an analogy between 'authoritative utterances' and requests (both provide source-based and content-independent reasons for action[8]), he writes:

---

[1] See HLA Hart, *The Concept of Law* (Oxford,1961), 27, 39.

[2] *Ibid* at 38–39.

[3] *Ibid* at 39.

[4] See also *ibid* at 39, ('these . . . rules make provision for the breakdown or failure of the primary purpose of the system'), 40.

[5] M Dan-Cohen, 'In Defence of Defiance' (1994) 23 *Philosophy and Public Affairs* 24.

[6] *Ibid* at 26. The term 'coercion' is somewhat misleading in this context, as not all legal threats are coercive. On what makes a threat coercive see J Raz, *The Morality of Freedom* (Oxford, 1986) 148–49. This point will be resumed later in this chapter.

[7] Above n 5, at 29 (the 'additive' conception is Hart's).

[8] *Ibid* at 27–28.

Consider a simple request such as 'Please pass the salt.' By making such a request A provides B with a reason . . . to pass the salt. Now suppose that A expands on his request by adding the words 'or else I'll break your arm.' On the additive view, B is now presented with two reasons for passing the salt: the reason generated by the initial request and the reason created by the coercive threat. But this analysis is strikingly inadequate. Rather than leaving the first reason intact, the threat clearly seems to undercut the request and to supersede it: the reason that B had to pass the salt prior to the threat has been destroyed by A's threat. . . . That A's threat does not simply outweigh the reason for passing the salt created by A's request, but rather nullifies it, seems clear. 'A request backed by a sanction' is an oxymoron.[9]

Something, it should be conceded, seems strange about the utterance 'Please pass the salt, or else I'll break your arm.' We should suspect, however, that this strangeness reflects a quality which is typical of requests but not of authoritative utterances; a quality which, unlike being source-based and content-independent, *differentiates* requests from typical authoritative utterances rather than forms part of their common denominator. The point can be put thus. A request is normally meant to be a reason for the addressee to do as requested, but not (or, at any rate, not necessarily) a reason not to act for other reasons—not an *exclusionary* reason for action.[10] The non-exclusionary nature of requests is the main difference between a request and, say, a command: the latter, but not the former, is normally intended not only as a reason for action, but also as a reason not to act for (certain) other reasons.[11] Now threats, too, are intended to create reasons for action for their addressees. These reasons may be described as negative and indirect. A threat creates a reason to embark on a course of action through making the possibility of following conflicting reasons (in ways which would amount to non-compliance) less desirable than it would have otherwise been. In this sense, although the reasons which threats create are not exclusionary by nature, a threat can be understood as 'directed against' conflicting reasons, as an attempt to undercut them, to diminish their motivating force. This, I believe, explains what is strange about attaching a threat to a request. It is specifically the latter's non-exclusionary nature that is at odds with the threat; it is the combination of a non-exclusionary reason and an expression of intention to bring about unwanted consequences if the addressee fails to act on it, that produces something that sounds (almost) like an oxymoron. At any rate it suggests that the person making the utterance does not really intend its first part to be taken as a request—in which case the word 'please' (as in the salt-passing example) appears patently out of context, thus making the utterance as a whole seem strange indeed.

[9] *Ibid* at 28–29.
[10] The terminology is Raz's. See discussion below on threats and exclusionary reasons.
[11] See J Raz, *Practical Reason and Norms* (2nd edn, Princeton, 1990), especially at 83–84, 100–1. See also *The Morality of Freedom*, above n 6, at 37. For a slightly different analysis see C Gans, *Philosophical Anarchism and Political Disobedience* (Cambridge, 1992) at 23–24.

The same argument can also explain why an utterance combining a request and threat would sound doubly oxymoronic, if that is possible, when the threat in question is coercive—and the threat in the salt-passing example *is* coercive. On a descriptive level, the difference between a coercive and a non-coercive threat is a matter of degree. It has to do with how weighty a reason against non-compliance is the consequence that the threat consists of communicating an intention to bring about. Loosely stated, for a threat to be considered coercive this should be a reason of overwhelming weight relative to conflicting reasons. It is in this sense (and not usually in the literal one) that, when referring to someone who did something as a result of being presented with a coercive threat, we say things like 'he had no choice.' And requests are not normally meant to achieve a similar effect.[12]

Requests, however, are not the most typical example of 'authoritative utterances', definitely not of the kind found in criminal law. Commands are. And given that, unlike requests, commands are normally intended as exclusionary reasons, it is not surprising to see that there is nothing intuitively erroneous or oxymoronic in the combination of a command and a threat. Dropping the 'please' in the original example is all the modification needed in order to illustrate this point. If the resulting 'Pass the salt or else I'll break your arm' still sounds incongruous or unreasonable, this is so not because of the disjunctive relationship between the command and the threat, but rather because of the remarkable lack of proportion between the significance of the required action (and, consequently, the apparent severity of a failure to comply) and the magnitude of the threatened sanction (breaking one's arm). Think, then, of another utterance: 'Pass the salt or else I won't pass you the pepper.' Is it clear here that the threat *nullifies* whatever normative force the first part of the utterance would have had had it stood alone?[13]

The disjunctive view, we may conclude, holds no obvious intuitive appeal in the context of cases where a threat is added to a command (nor, we may suspect, where it is added to any other type of reason for action that similarly purports to have an exclusionary force). Dan-Cohen's main concern, however, is with such cases. He tries to establish that the disjunctive view applies to them just as much as it applies to requests. Let us now examine in turn the arguments introduced in support of this thesis.

---

[12] Requests sometimes achieve, either intentionally or not, an effect similar to that which coercive threats are intended to achieve. Some requests 'cannot be refused.' But such cases owe their explanation to special circumstances, and not to the nature of requests in general.

[13] Dan-Cohen observes, and to my mind correctly, that the constraints on the harshness of the threats authorities tend to issue, normally in the shape of some proportion between the severity of an offence and its punishment, reflect considerations external to the logic of threats as such (see above n 5, at 27). Yet here it is necessary to think of a case where such proportion exists, in order to ensure that the intuitive response to the example is indeed a response to the combination of a command and a threat, and not to the harshness of the threat itself.

Threats and Expressive Reasons

When an authority issues a directive, so goes the first argument, it creates an opportunity for its addressees to express, through obedience, an attitude of respect (or, as Dan-Cohen puts it, deference) towards the authority. Obeying a command (or, similarly, carrying out a request) is a way of demonstrating the fact that the command was taken as a content-independent reason for action. When the command is accompanied by a threat, however, the opportunity is destroyed. In the presence of a threat:

> compliance can no longer carry the significance it otherwise would have had as an expression of respect. For all we know—and this includes the agent herself—compliance was motivated by fear of sanction, and is therefore devoid of expressive content.[14]

This argument, while capturing an important truth, is exaggerated to an extent that threatens to obscure this truth altogether. At least in certain contexts threats can, indeed, seriously undermine an otherwise significant opportunity to express attitudes through action. Moreover, the effect of undermining actions' expressive potential that certain threats are likely to have may indeed be greater than the equivalent effect that (the presence of) other reasons for action which are devoid of expressive content would normally have. (I shall return to these thoughts at a later stage.) Now how significant an opportunity to express respect for authority criminal law would provide if not for the threats it issues is itself contentious: clearly in this particular context it would almost always be questionable, even in the absence of any threat, whether and to what extent obedience should be understood as an expression of respect. Much more troublesome, however, is Dan-Cohen's contention that whenever compliance could be explained as motivated by the threat, it could not possibly be explained otherwise. This is so, he maintains, since threats are clearly announced (unlike various other 'non-expressive' reasons or motives, the existence of which can only be suspected), and since threats are designed to provide reasons for compliance all by themselves (unlike other reasons or motives, the role of which is 'both speculative and variable').[15]

Threats are, indeed, typically clearly announced (notably when employed by the law); and *coercive* threats, at least, are indeed designed to provide reasons for action strong enough to induce it without the aid of other reasons for the same action (and, moreover, despite the possible presence of conflicting reasons). These facts, as I shall later acknowledge, are not irrelevant in assessing the special way in which (certain kinds of) threats can prevent actions from fulfilling an expressive function; yet they fall well short of establishing that once a threat has been issued, it is necessarily the threat and nothing else that must be

---

[14] Above n 5, at 38.
[15] *Ibid* at 39.

viewed as, let alone be, the motivating force behind the agent's compliance. This suggestion is particularly dubious in cases where the threat in question is a reason to refrain from doing something that the agent may well not wish to do anyway, rather than a reason to do something that the agent is not likely to be inclined to do otherwise—and note that the former, rather than the latter, is the case with most of the threats made by criminal law. English law, to take one example, designates a punishment specifically for those who profane corpses. The threat is clearly announced, and, it is reasonable to assume, designed to provide a strong enough reason to refrain from profaning corpses, strong enough not only for those who can find no single other reason for so refraining, but also for those who might be, for whatever reason, predisposed to profane corpses. Yet to suggest that for all we know, let alone for all *they* know, English people's compliance with the prohibition on the profanation of corpses is motivated by fear of sanction seems somewhat far-fetched.

Of course there is nothing wrong with arguing that refraining from the profanation of corpses in England is devoid of expressive content. For rather obvious reasons, it would still be devoid of expressive content even if the rule that prohibits it were not accompanied by a (powerful, clearly announced) threat. It is true that some legal requirements could provide a better opportunity than this—a reasonably good opportunity, even—for expressing deference through compliance if not for the threat attached to them (again, the likely candidates would mostly be positive requirements, eg to pay taxes, rather than prohibitions of the kind that dominate penal codes). The fact that obedience to the law is a very imperfect medium for expressing deference to begin with (as Dan-Cohen himself acknowledges[16]) does not invalidate this claim. A threat does add one more possible reason and one more possible explanation for compliance, thus making it harder, both for the agent and for her intended audience (the authority itself, other people), to attach symbolic significance to compliance. And the stronger a reason for compliance and the more likely an explanation for compliance the threat appears to be—variables for which the severity of the threatened sanction, the extent to which the threat is publicly and clearly announced, and the likelihood that it will be carried out upon non-compliance, are all relevant factors—the more we have a reason to blame the difficulty to convey deference through compliance on the threat's presence. *This* proposition, however, fails to provide any substantial support for the disjunctive view. The potential expressive quality of compliance may be considered a desirable advantage that *uniquely* employing the normative method could offer, and this advantage may indeed be compromised, or even lost altogether, when the normative method is employed alongside threats. Accordingly, it could be said that a certain price is paid for the (undisputed) fact that the law does not employ normativity alone—that it is not, if you like, *purely* normative. But there is nothing

---

[16] 'Mixed motives are common, and there is always the possibility that other reasons motivated compliance—a possibility that inevitably detracts from the clarity of the signal conveyed': *ibid.*

here to link the notion that such a price is paid to the notion that the law cannot be understood as normative in any way. In a single effort to establish such a link, Dan-Cohen points out that the loss of the expressive quality of compliance also removes the corresponding reason for obeying authority.[17] Even so, the conclusion remains the same, for normativity does not in any way hinge on the reason which is thus removed: normativity can perhaps be understood, in the legal context at any rate, as requiring obedience *out of* deference, but not necessarily *in order to express* deference.

Threats and Trust

Dan-Cohen's second argument follows a similar logic to that of the first, this time focusing on what he calls 'the importance of being trusted.' An authority's call for compliance can be seen as an expression of trust in its addressees. It enables the agent '[to score] points on a scoreboard that is of significance to him,'[18] by proving, through compliance, that he is trustworthy. But then:

> [A]ll this is possible only insofar as the authority's appeal is not backed by threats. When it is, the authority can no longer be understood as trusting its subjects and relying on their goodwill. Obeying the authority, no matter how enthusiastically, will not serve to justify the authority's trust, simply because in the presence of coercive threats there is no trust to justify.[19]

As an attempt to establish the disjunctive view, this argument could apparently be rejected just as easily as the previous one. As with the case of creating an opportunity to express deference, both expressing trust (in the addressees) and creating an opportunity (for the addressees) to prove trustworthy could at best be understood as welcome side-effects of employing the normative method. If proving oneself trustworthy could (as Dan-Cohen suggests) itself serve as a reason for compliance, then that is another advantageous side-effect. Being side-effects, however, the loss of such advantages is not an indication that the authority does not create the kind of reasons that the normative method consists in creating, or that it does not expect its subjects to follow such reasons, or that it could not be obeyed for such reasons. Thus even if it is true that directives which are unaccompanied by threats can be understood as an expression of trust, and true that threats undercut or even nullify that expression—and with it the opportunity to prove trustworthy, and the reason for action that the desire to prove trustworthy may produce—nothing need be wrong with Hart's 'additive' view. Rather than challenging and offering an alternative to that view (which is, after all, what the disjunctive view purports to do), the argument amounts to no

---

[17] *Ibid.*
[18] *Ibid* at 40.
[19] *Ibid* at 41.

more than highlighting yet another implication of the fact that the additive view explicitly embraces, namely that the law is not purely normative.[20]

But I want to suggest that a modified version of the same argument could come closer, at least, to challenging the additive view. To do that, both of the argument's main propositions need to be taken a step further. As for the connection between normativity and trust, what needs to be shown is not just that employing the normative method can be understood as a manifestation of trust, but that it *requires* trust; that rather than merely creating an opportunity for the addressees to prove themselves trustworthy, it *presupposes* that they are. This step need not be too difficult to take, for if it is true that normativity can be understood as a manifestation of trust, this is so precisely because it normally requires or presupposes trust. As for the second proposition, what needs to be shown is that the use of threats does not only withdraw a positive message of trust which, if not for the threat, could be conveyed through the use of normativity, but that it indicates a fundamental *lack* of trust—indicates that the kind of trust which is a normal requirement for using normativity does not exist. The conjunction of the two modified propositions would still fall short of establishing that normativity and threats are logically incompatible, or that an utterance made in an attempt to put both into use simultaneously is an oxymoron. But it may cast doubt over the seriousness or the sincerity of such an utterance. It may suggest that an authority that issues threats does not really expect its subjects to act on the kind of reasons that the normative component of its call for compliance purports to create. And as we shall see, such a conclusion may suffice to put a question mark over the validity of Hart's understanding of the way the law operates as a means of guiding behaviour.

In what sense can the normative method be understood as requiring trust? To answer this question, let us first make sure that we have a clear grasp of what this method involves. We may start by classifying it as belonging to the broader category of methods of affecting behaviour through the intentional creation of reasons for action.[21] Other methods, however, such as issuing threats or offering inducements, could be similarly classified. What distinguishes the normative method from such other methods? Dan-Cohen characterises normativity as 'a matter of voluntary obedience.'[22] This is not helpful, if only for the fact that almost every conscious action—including actions taken in compliance with a coercive threat or in response to inducement—can, under some description, be viewed as voluntary. (Clear exceptions include actions which are physically forced upon the agent, or produced through some extreme form of manipulation.) But we need not look far for an answer, for the essence of the normative

---

[20] Note that the example around which Dan-Cohen builds the current argument, that of the 'honour system' of examinations (see *ibid* at 40), is a paradigmatic case of employing pure normativity.

[21] This formulation accommodates cases where reasons are created not through an act of communication. For present purposes, however, I will ignore such cases.

[22] Above n 5, at 26.

method is captured, albeit somewhat also obscured, in Hart's own account of criminal law's primary function.

Let us recall. Criminal law designates by rules certain types of behaviour as standards for the guidance of its subjects. The subjects are then 'expected without the aid or intervention of officials to understand the rules and to see that the rules apply to them and to conform to them.' Now it could be pointed out that even if the threat of a sanction and nothing else were expected to lead to conformity, and even if the law did not purport to create any other reason for conformity, conformity would still be expected to ensue without the aid or intervention of officials: after all, it is precisely when there is no need to carry it out that a threat proves successful as a means of guiding behaviour. The need to identify a breach and impose a sanction, in other words, could equally be viewed as a mark of failure both of the primary (normativity) and the secondary (threats) 'functions' of the law, which is why the 'without the aid or intervention' proviso may obscure the role which is assigned in Hart's account to 'standard-designating' rules of law, and consequently obscure the nature of normativity. These could be made clearer if Hart's account were read as follows: people are expected to understand the rules, see that they apply to them, and, *as a result*, conform to them. This formulation better highlights the notion that the normative method consists in intending the directive itself (be it a general rule, a particular command, a request, etc), the very fact that the performance of a certain action has been required, as a reason to perform that action—the directive itself, that is, as distinguished from (among other things, but crucially here) occurrences which compliance (as in the case of inducement) or non-compliance (as in the case of threats) are likely to bring about and which are not part of what justifies the authority in issuing the directive and demanding compliance in the first place.[23]

For a directive to be a reason in itself to do as directed, something must justify considering it as such; something which is not usually explicit in the directive must justify the call for compliance it embodies, and render valid the reason which the directive purports to be. A command (or a request, etc) which is issued in the absence of something which could potentially, at least, justify the notion that it should be taken as a reason to do as commanded, is not only likely to prove ineffective as a means of affecting the addressee's behaviour. Its failure to invoke any such justification is likely to render it utterly preposterous, and the act of issuing it eccentric.[24] (Think of a request to pass the salt when the person

---

[23] This last qualification is meant to distinguish an occurrence such as the broken arm in the salt-passing example from an occurrence such as getting richer in the case of following the advice of a stock-broker. The fact that the stock-broker's advice is likely to make the person who acts on it richer is not only a reason to follow the advice, but also what justifies the broker in giving the advice and in expecting her client to follow it.

[24] That explains why every de facto authority must claim or at least be held by others to be a legitimate authority as well. (On this feature of political authorities see eg Raz, above n 6, at 23–28, and *The Authority of Law* (Oxford, 1979) ch 1.)

who makes it can clearly reach the salt more easily than the addressee, or of a person giving orders to strangers she bumps into in the street.) The precise nature of the required justification may of course vary considerably when different kinds of authority (or source from which a directive emanates) and different kinds of directive are considered. But in general it can be said that every instance of employing the normative method can be understood as encompassing an implicit reference to an existing justification, and an invitation to the addressee to acknowledge that justification and, by treating the directive as a reason, act on it.[25]

We can now see one sense in which the use of the normative method can be said to require trust. In certain contexts, at least, it largely depends for its efficacy on the addressee(s) formulating and acting on a judgment which is potentially, and quite typically, the product of rather sophisticated reasoning. Indeed, the characteristic intricacy of the kind of considerations that could support the call for compliance made by political authorities clearly marks the use of the normative method by such authorities as one such context.[26] And a belief in a person's capacity to formulate correctly, and disposition to act on, such judgments is itself a very significant sense of trusting. Thus inasmuch as employing a method of affecting behaviour can be understood as related to a belief in that method's likelihood to achieve its aims, reliance (by a political authority) on the normative method can be understood to require, and consequently to manifest, trust in the addressees.[27]

Now we can also see why the addition of a threat is likely to undercut significantly that message of trust which the use of the normative method could other-

---

[25] Inviting or expecting the addressee to *acknowledge* the justification need not amount to expecting her to consciously conceive it as such in her deliberation. The formulation adopted here and later in the text is intended to accommodate more than one way in which normative considerations may impinge on a person's deliberation and affect her action. For an insightful account of (at least some of) the different possibilities see S Scheffler, *Human Morality* (Oxford, 1992) ch 3, especially at 30–32.

[26] Note that this intricacy characterises not only considerations which in fact justify obedience (are there any?), but, crucially, also considerations of the kind that may be thought or are commonly thought to do so, but ultimately fail.

[27] Of course, the use of a method of affecting behaviour need not always be understood as reflecting a belief in that method's effectiveness in the circumstances. An authority (or a person) may employ a certain method while not entertaining such a belief at all, or while merely hoping, perhaps for no good reason, that it will prove effective, etc. A further possibility that can frustrate the suggested link between normativity and trust is that of employing a certain method while believing (or hoping) that compliance will ensue but for a different reason than that which the method in question is usually designed to create. An authority may assume, for instance, that its addressees will abide by its commands because they are irrational conformists, and thus regardless of any awareness on their part of a moral obligation to obey. (Could such an authority be said to trust its addressees? Is it conceptually possible to *trust* someone to behave irrationally? Whatever the answer—and I will touch on this question at a later stage—that would be a very different sense of trust than that alluded to in the text.) It is in light of the possibility of such cases that it can only be said that the normative method *normally* requires trust, a proposition that reflects the assumption that the use of a certain method of affecting behaviour is normally accompanied by the belief that it will achieve its intended aim (compliance), and achieve it in the way in which it is designed and usually meant to achieve it.

wise be understood to convey. Inasmuch as using the normative method can be said to require, and thus also manifest, trust, supplementing it with *any* additional method of affecting behaviour would tend to undercut such a manifestation, simply by highlighting the authority's awareness of the possibility that using the normative method alone may not secure compliance. At least this is true when the additional method used does not require trust in a similar way— and this is clearly the case with threats. Justifiability does not play in the context of using threats an equivalent role to that which it plays in the context of using the normative method. For a threat to be effective, the authority issuing it need not be legitimate nor even claim legitimacy. Nothing need justify the threat, the act of issuing it, or indeed the very endeavour to affect the addressee's behaviour in the first place that the threat serves. All that the threat-issuing authority needs to do is make sure that the consequence it attaches to non-compliance is something the addressee would wish to avoid, and wish to avoid sufficiently; and identifying that consequence as such, on the addressee's part, need not, and normally does not, involve the kind of potentially complex, abstract normative reasoning on which the efficacy of the normative method typically depends.[28]

Precisely the same argument, it might be noted, applies to certain other methods of affecting behaviour, inducement for instance. Inducement need not normally require trust any more (or in a deeper, more meaningful sense) than threats, and at any rate not as much or in the same sense as normativity. Trust itself, however, can be a matter of degree; it is not all or nothing. And trust and circumspection are not mutually exclusive. For the challenge to the 'additive' view to materialise, a stronger claim regarding the nature of threats needs to be established. Is there anything about threats to suggest that using them is in any way *incompatible* with the kind of trust that the normative method requires, or that they are particularly unlikely to be used when this kind of trust obtains? This brings us to the second necessary modification to the argument with which we started in this section.

It could be pointed out, for a start, that by resorting to the use of threats, an authority simply gives a clearer, more conspicuous indication of its awareness of the possibility of non-compliance compared to a case where, say, it offers inducements. This is so because whereas the inducement is attached to compliance, a threat directly invokes the possibility of, and attaches a consequence to, non-compliance. And whereas the inducement can sometimes be interpreted as an expression of gratitude (wholly or partly), the precise function of the adverse consequence of non-compliance that the threat describes, or indeed the function of the threat itself, is usually rather unambiguous.

A related but farther-reaching argument suggests that threats are offensive by nature. Note, first, that in certain contexts the very existence of doubt—the very

---

[28] It is possible to conceive of a threat that would depend for its efficacy on the addressee's capacity for abstract moral reasoning ('If you don't stop singing I'll treat people as means rather than ends'). The point, however, is that there is nothing in the logic or the practice of using threats to suggest that this would normally be the case.

fact that a distinct possibility of non-compliance is perceived—can be offensive to the person whose compliance is at stake. In such cases, a threat is likely to be offensive simply by virtue of being, as we have just seen, a rather vivid and unambiguous reminder of the existence of such doubt. But threats can be said to be offensive in a more significant sense. To make a threat is to communicate the intention to bring about, under certain conditions (non-compliance), a consequence which is (or is thought to be) something the addressee would wish to avoid. This consequence is stipulated precisely as such: out of awareness that, and at least partly because, it would be to the addressee's dislike (or discomfort, or contrary to the addressee's real or perceived interests, etc). And the point is that in the very willingness to bring about such a consequence, or the very expression of a willingness to do so, there is something offensive or disrespectful. Just how offensive a given threat is, would depend on the interplay between numerous considerations, some bearing directly on the threat itself (the nature of the required action, the nature of the threatened action, the proportion between the two, the relevance of the threatened action to the required action,[29] etc), and some related to the circumstances of making it. But it can reasonably be argued that, subject to a great deal of variation in degree, there is something potentially offensive in the very act of issuing a threat, in the very expression of a willingness to act deliberately against the addressee's preferences or interests.[30]

More could be said in pursuit of this line of argument. Indeed, one of the most important distinctions to be drawn in evaluating the offensiveness of threats, that between coercive and non-coercive threats, has yet to be discussed. But what has been said thus far, supplemented with a simple assumption of practical rationality, suffices in order for the touted challenge to the additive view to take shape. The assumption is that in the absence of a special reason to do otherwise, rational agencies prefer not to offend others. If threats are offensive by nature, the implication is that, other things being equal, rational agencies would not normally resort to using them as long as they believe that the same could be achieved by means which are not, or are less, offensive. A belief that a person's behaviour could, in given circumstances, be governed normatively, or the existence of the kind of trust that such a belief normally reflects, thus appear to be at odds with the willingness to resort to the use of threats in order to govern that person's behaviour.

Such a conclusion, as I said at the outset, still falls short of lending support to the proposition that 'a norm backed by a threat' presents any *logical* incongruity

---

[29] Sometimes such relevance can render a threat less offensive (in the sense discussed here), that is, in cases where the threatened action is somehow a natural or an obvious response to non-compliance (as in, for instance, 'If you don't drive carefully I won't let you borrow my car').

[30] This is not to deny that issuing a threat may sometimes be in the addressee's interest or for the addressee's own good (in which case, incidentally, the threat should be considerably less offensive than otherwise). But in any case, in order for the threat to serve as a reason for compliance, the consequence of non-compliance it describes must be something the addressee would wish, or perceive to be in her interests, to avoid.

(if only because the tension exposed is merely in terms of the *normal* conditions for the use of the normative method and for the use of threats), yet its implications for Hart's view may seem grave nevertheless. Typically, the only method of affecting behaviour which is explicit in criminal law is that of issuing threats: penal codes, after all, tend to look like price lists, not guidebooks. Thus, for criminal law to be understood as making use of the normative method, it should be possible to *infer*, as Hart does, the existence of the appropriate expectation: that people will extract rules from the threats and treat these rules as reasons for compliance. According to the argument thus far, however, a willingness to issue threats indicates that such an expectation does not really exist. If the argument applies, then Hart's account of the way criminal law operates, while not logically unfeasible, must be fictitious.

It should not be hard to see, however, that the argument, although sound, does not apply. Ascribing intentions, expectations, or attitudes to abstract entities such as the law or the state is, analytically, a risky business. One error that can lead to distortion consists in the failure to take into account the myriad of special circumstances and considerations that inform the operation of the state (or, similarly, any other authority). The law, or the state through the law, aims to guide the behaviour of society as a whole. Its subjects are many, and are potentially and usually highly heterogeneous. For this reason alone it would be fanciful to perceive the law as displaying the kind of attitude that normally accompanies the use of threats in more or less intimate, inter-personal contexts, as a unified attitude towards its subjects as a whole.

Anticipating an argument to this effect—let us call it 'the argument from the multiplicity of subjects'—Dan-Cohen dismisses it as follows:

> It might be thought that the state addresses its threats only to recalcitrant citizens, while speaking in purely normative terms to the law-abiding ones. But this would be a delusion. No matter how small the number of recalcitrant citizens because of whom coercion is employed, *given the generality of the law* everyone's behaviour falls within the scope of the threats.[31]

Of course the state does not speak in 'purely normative terms' to anyone—not through penal codes, at any rate; but the argument from the multiplicity of subjects does not depend on the notion (nor does it suggest) that it does. And the generality of the law, or specifically the fact that legal threats apply to everyone, would only be a reason to ascribe to the state an attitude of sweeping distrust of its citizens if this mode of operation could not be explained, or explained more plausibly, as the product of something different altogether. And surely it could more plausibly be explained as reflecting some of the special considerations which apply to the state (and potentially, in varying degrees, to other practical authorities) as an organ which is expected to guide, control, and co-ordinate the behaviour of a multiplicity of subjects, and to do so in keeping with exacting

---

[31] Above n 5, at 49, n 40 (emphasis added).

standards of efficiency and fairness. The greater plausibility of such an explanation, combined with the popularity of the belief that *some* people's conformity
with certain standards can only be achieved through the use of threats, is evident
in the fact that most people do not take offence at being personally regarded by
their state or their law-makers as potential perpetrators of each and every activity to which the penal code attaches a threat. Indeed, if criminal law were seriously taken to manifest some unified perception of the citizenry as a whole, not
only the use of threats but in some cases (the profanation of corpses, surely?) the
very fact that a standard has been spelt out would cause widespread offence.

As the argument from the multiplicity of subjects does not apply in the context of the relationship between individuals (or, at any rate, between parties
to contract), the argument it served to reject should be revisited when the focus
of the discussion shifts away from the relationship between authority and its
subjects. But before that, two more arguments that were made in the latter context in support of the disjunctive view need to be considered.

The Willingness to Assume the Risk of Disobedience

Dan-Cohen's next argument is similar in its intended implications to the argument I outlined (and the applicability of which I ultimately rejected) in the previous section, this time focusing not on trust but on the allegedly required
willingness to assume the risk of disobedience. The argument is developed
through an analogy with gifts. '[T]he concept of a gift,' he observes, 'involves as
one of its essential properties the donor's freedom to either give or withhold a
particular object.'[32] Accordingly, one can be said seriously to want an object *as
a gift* only if one wants the object subject to that property, that is as something
which the donor freely chooses to give. The 'seriously' proviso is meant to
exclude a hypothetical preference on which the agent is in fact unwilling to act.
It is satisfied 'when the benefits of getting a desired object by way of the donor's
free choice outweigh the risk of not getting the object at all'—a proposition that
would clearly be negated if one resorts to the use of a coercive threat in order to
obtain it.[33] The analogy with authority is then drawn straightforwardly:

> As with the gift example, authority's readiness to impose upon its subjects the man-
> dated behaviour undermines its capacity to make a credible appeal to voluntary obe-
> dience because it reveals authority's unwillingness to assume the risk, inherent in the
> very concept of obedience, that disobedience might ensue.[34]

[32] Above n 5, at 43.
[33] *Ibid* at 42–43.
[34] *Ibid* at 43–44. The notion that what distinguishes normativity is the voluntariness of the obedience it calls for was dismissed earlier, but the current argument does not depend on this notion for
its validity: its conclusion could be read as a rejection of the idea that an authority that uses threats
can be understood as attempting to affect behaviour normatively, in the sense of intending its directives themselves to be taken as reasons to do as directed.

But the analogy is misleading. The option of disobedience is not inherent in the concept of obedience to the commands of an authority in the same way that the option of not giving the gift can be said to be inherent in the concept of a gift, and a willingness to assume the risk of disobedience is not an essential feature of employing the normative method in the same sense or to the same extent that a willingness to assume the risk of not receiving the gift is linked to the notion of wanting something *as* a gift. The dis-analogy here is similar in its logic to the dis-analogy which was exposed earlier between requests and commands; but I wish to take the opportunity to make a somewhat different point this time.

It should be noted, first, that there is something deceptive in talking about 'a willingness to assume *the risk*,' because it could be taken to imply that the risk involved—and accordingly the willingness to assume it—is a matter of all or nothing, whereas in fact it is not: the risk can be a matter of degree, it can be reduced without necessarily being eliminated, and one may be willing, or even required, to assume some but not all of it, or allowed to take certain actions but not others in attempting to reduce it. Indeed, even in the context of wanting a gift, certain actions which could be taken in order to reduce the risk of not receiving it are plainly not at odds with the notion of (seriously) wanting *a gift*: reminding someone that tomorrow is your birthday, for instance, or letting it be known that the possession of a certain object would really make you happy. Now the distinction between measures that are and measures that are not acceptable, in a given context, as means of reducing the risk that a person will act other than desired, is in part a reflection of the kind of freedom which the person whose action is at stake is supposed to enjoy in taking that action. And gift-giving and obedience to political authorities (or obeying commands in general) are markedly different in this respect. The freedom that the concept of a gift is normally understood to involve—the freedom with which the decision whether or not to give a gift is normally assumed and expected to be taken—is not just freedom from physical coercion or from extreme forms of manipulation or psychological pressure. It is a comprehensive moral freedom, one that includes the freedom to ignore valid reasons for giving the gift or to follow most (if not all) kinds of conflicting reason. Indeed, even in circumstances where not giving a gift would be considered downright rude, it would not normally be considered morally wrong.

This explains why the use of threats is at odds with the notion of wanting a gift, whereas the other two examples of risk-reducing measures mentioned in the previous paragraph are not. The latter can be understood as attempts to ensure that the agent is aware of existing reasons to give a gift, or, as in the case of divulging how very happy the donee would be to receive a particular gift, to ensure that she is aware of the full force or the full significance of some such reasons. As such they do not—not directly and not necessarily, at any rate—call into question the would-be donor's moral freedom not to give the gift. The use of a threat, by contrast, strongly suggests a failure to acknowledge this very moral freedom. It signals that the option of not giving the gift is conceived as somehow

illegitimate. (A threat is not usually intended to provide its addressee with a genuine choice; to issue a threat is not just to fix a price on a prospective course of
action, but to try to create a reason for not embarking on it.) This does not mean,
of course, that once faced with a threat the donor could not *give* a gift: after all
the donee's attitude or understanding of the situation need not affect the donor's,
and (unlike the donor's attitude) is not in itself part of the very concept of a gift.
But it does indicate that as far as the person who issues the threat is concerned,
the matter at stake, the required action, is not really gift-giving.

The dis-analogy with commands is now plain to see. The concept of a command does not involve the kind of freedom (whether or not to obey) that the
concept of a gift involves (whether or not to give). Commands are intended not
only as reasons that the addressee is not free to ignore, but also as reasons not
to act for certain (and sometimes, as is typically the case with commands issued
by political authorities, *all*) other reasons. And since issuing a command is perfectly compatible with claiming obedience to be the only legitimate course of
action, the 'de-legitimising' connotation of threats does not in any way mark
them out as inappropriate means by which to reduce the risk that the command
will be disobeyed. Similarly, the fact that a command is accompanied by an
additional, intentionally-created reason to obey, need not indicate that the command itself is not intended to be (or not genuinely hoped to prove) a sufficient
reason for the addressee to do as commanded, and need not prevent the
addressee from actually taking it as such.

This is not to say that the use of every conceivable means of reducing the risk
of non-compliance is compatible with the kind of call for compliance that commands are usually understood to embody, or with the very notion of a command
as something that can be *obeyed*. A command may be intended to provide the
addressee with but one legitimate choice, and may be reinforced by a threat so
that obedience is rendered by far and away the addressee's most desirable (or
least undesirable) choice; but the concept of obedience (at least in the sense in
which it typically features in discussions of political authorities and their relationship with their subjects) still calls for the addressee to *make* that choice.
'Obedience,' that is, implies an action which is the product of a conscious decision, an action which can count as the agent's in more than a nominal sense.[35]
This admittedly is a rather crude characterisation of the kind of freedom that
authoritative directives which represent or embody a call for obedience entail;
the point, however, is that this freedom is, conceptually speaking, highly limited, and accordingly that very few measures by which the risk of disobedience
may be reduced—measures such as the application of physical force or extreme
manipulation—in fact have the effect of altogether denying it.

---

[35] It may not be conceptually wrong to use the term 'obedience' when describing, say, compliance
with the instructions of a hypnotist while under deep hypnosis. But this kind of obedience is clearly
different from obedience in the sense that commands are normally characterised as calling and providing an opportunity for, and at any rate different from the kind of obedience that political authorities normally call for.

To conclude, the use of threats to supplement an authoritative directive does not amount to a refusal to assume a risk which is inherent in the concept of obedience. In my refutation of this argument, I talked about threats in general, not necessarily coercive ones. It is worth emphasising, however, that whereas the use of *any* threat in order to obtain something calls into questions the notion that the object is wanted *as a gift*, when it comes to commands (or similar authoritative directives) not even the use of coercive threats poses the equivalent problem. Coercive threats may indeed reduce the risk that disobedience may ensue to a bare minimum, yet unlike some other forms of coercion which are not at all aimed at producing conscious decisions, their use does not normally have, and is not normally intended to achieve, the effect of denying their addressees the opportunity to *obey* the directive that they accompany.[36]

Threats and Exclusionary Reasons

The fact that has been mentioned in passing in discussing previous arguments, namely that commands are intended as exclusionary reasons, is at the centre of Dan-Cohen's final argument.[37] Here it is this feature of commands that is claimed to render them incompatible with threats, so that an authority which uses threats 'can be estopped through its own behaviour from claiming exclusionary force for its demands.'[38] The estoppel is based on the notion that by using threats, an authority ventures to create reasons of the kind that exclusionary reasons aim at excluding.

The notion that holds this argument together is that exclusionary reasons exclude by kind. If an exclusionary reason excludes economic reasons, for instance, it marks such reasons out as inappropriate grounds for action regardless (among other things[39]) of whether they happen to be reasons for or against doing what the exclusionary reason is a reason for. Now the commands of political authorities, like all exclusionary reasons, usually purport to exclude (among other things) their addressees' present desires;[40] and while 'practically speaking' an authority should only be concerned with excluding reasons *against* compliance, 'the logic of authority's normative appeal does not allow

---

[36] A threat may at times have the effect of confusing, intimidating, or overwhelming its addressee so much as to prompt involuntary action, but that indeed is not the normal effect of threats, nor the effect they are normally intended to achieve.

[37] Dan-Cohen writes that 'authority intends its commands to be not just first-order reasons to act as commanded but also second-order, "exclusionary," reasons to ignore at least some reasons that would otherwise apply to the agent and might counsel disobedience' (above n 5, at 44). Exclusionary reasons, however (as Raz made clear in the postscript to the second edition of *Practical Reason and Norms*, above n 11, especially at 182–86), are not reasons *to ignore* other reasons, but reasons *not to act for* other reasons—and I shall use the term to mean this in what follows. This confusion does not affect the rest of Dan-Cohen's argument.

[38] Above n 5, at 49.

[39] Regardless in particular of the excluded reason's weight. (See Raz, *The Authority of Law*, above n 24, at 22.)

[40] Above n 5, at 44–45 (and see Dan-Cohen's reference to Raz, there).

for such selectivity.'[41] Threats, however, are meant to enlist their addressees' present desires (the desire to escape the threatened 'sanction') as a reason for compliance. On that basis Dan-Cohen contends that '[a]n appeal by authority to its subjects' supportive inclinations to the exclusion of the hostile ones'—something that would be 'unprincipled and self-contradictory'—is 'precisely what an authority does when it backs its orders by coercive threats.'[42]

Yet it is not. The appeal to supportive inclinations (if the threat may be described in this way) is not, in itself, to the exclusion of hostile ones. A threat does not *exclude* other reasons at all. All a threat can do is counter the weight of, or at best outweigh, the reasons or inclinations against which it is pitched. If there is an exclusionary component in the authority's 'appeal,' it is not the threat but the command or the rule that the threat accompanies or that could be extracted from the threat—and *this rule* is indeed meant to exclude all inclinations (and other reasons), both supportive of and hostile to compliance. If no rule or command could be extracted from legal threats, then the 'appeal' in question would indeed hold no exclusionary force and could not be understood as claiming such force (and the authority making it could not be understood as employing the normative method). But none of the arguments examined thus far has established this to be the case, and there seems to be no reason for simply assuming that it is. On the contrary, the thrust of much of the discussion thus far has gone directly against such an assumption.

The combined message which can be extracted from a conjunction of a command and a threat is that acting on any inclination would be inappropriate, whereas acting on 'hostile' inclinations—as well as acting for (some or all) other reasons which conflict with the command—will carry a penalty. There is nothing unprincipled or contradictory about that. The addition of a threat can be understood as indicative of awareness of the possibility that the exclusionary component might fail to achieve its practical aim—that the exclusionary reason might not be taken and followed as such—and as an attempt to ensure that even in such a case, compliance would ensue. This, in fact, is precisely the role ascribed to threats in the 'additive' view.[43] By fulfilling this role the threat does not invalidate the exclusionary reason nor strip it of its exclusionary force.[44]

---

[41] Above n 5, at 47.

[42] *Ibid.*

[43] As Hart put it, 'the rules requiring the courts to impose the sanctions in the event of disobedience . . . make provision for the breakdown or failure of the primary purpose of the system' (above n 1, at 39). Again it could be pointed out that Hart's previously quoted formulation—'Only when the law is broken, and [the] primary function of the law fails'—somewhat conceals the relationship between the normative (primary) function and the use of threats: if the normative function consists in introducing rules and intending them as (exclusionary) reasons for compliance, then this function fails not only when the law is broken but, albeit less visibly, whenever people do not treat the rules as intended, ie as exclusionary reasons (and even if they do not break the law).

[44] In certain circumstances, the fact that a 'Do X or else . . .' threat has been issued may provide a reason *against* X-ing, perhaps even strong enough to outweigh (some or all) existing reasons for X-ing (for instance, when issuing the threat was in one way or another inappropriate, and noncompliance is an effective way of registering an objection, or preventing a recurrence of such conduct, or asserting one's freedom, etc). But that, clearly, is not true of threats in general.

II. NORMATIVITY AND THREATS IN PERSONAL RELATIONS

Despite the fact that it draws on a number of important insights, as a thesis pertaining to the relationship between authority and its subjects the disjunctive view fails. The argument that came closest to challenging the competing 'additive' view, however, was rejected on the basis of a consideration—the multiplicity of subjects—that usually does not apply in the context of personal relations. And as our interest lies, ultimately, in such relations, I would like to revisit that argument and investigate it a bit further.

The argument in question revealed a certain tension between the attitudes that normally accompany the use of normativity and the use of threats, thus suggesting what we may call a 'second-order incompatibility' between these two methods of affecting behaviour. The operative propositions in this argument were, on the one hand, the notion that the normative method normally requires trust, and, on the other, the offensive nature of threats. I will comment on the kind of trust that the normative method requires at the beginning of the next chapter. In connection with the second proposition, I wish to comment now on the distinction between coercive and non-coercive threats.

Coercive and Non-Coercive Threats

I mentioned before that the distinction between coercive and non-coercive threats is relevant in assessing their offensiveness, and in examining the compatibility of their use with the use of the normative method. The first thing to notice about this distinction is that it cannot be drawn in purely descriptive terms.[45] Unlike in a case where, for instance, a person's finger is physically forced to pull the trigger, when a coercive threat is used its addressee is put in a position where she can, and has to, choose what to do. It is something about the nature of the choice it offers that justifies the classification of a threat as coercive, and justifies seeing the person who faces this choice as being coerced to act in a certain way. Such a justification cannot be the product of a strictly descriptive account of the situation since it must involve the two-fold evaluative task of expounding the normative significance of coercion and, in correlation, assessing the comparative weight of the reasons for and against each of the options the coerced (or not) person has.[46]

[45] See Raz, above n 6.
[46] The fact that this evaluative task is two-fold in the way described explains how it is possible that from one viewpoint on the normative significance of coercion, threatening to bring about a certain consequence, C, in order to prevent Q from doing A may count as a coercive threat, whereas threatening to bring about C in order to prevent Q from doing something else, B, may not.

The descriptive core of coercion by threats is captured in the following formulation:[47]

P subjects Q to a coercive threat not to do A only if
(1) P communicates to Q that he intends to bring about some consequence, C, if Q does A.
(2) P makes this communication intending Q to believe that he does so in order to get Q not to do A.
(3) That C will happen is, for Q, a reason of great weight for not doing A.
(4) Q believes that it is likely that P will bring about C if Q does A and that C would leave him worse off, having done A, than if he did not do A and P did not bring about C.

To get a formulation of the speech act 'to threaten,' we need to look at conditions (1)–(3), subject to two changes. The words 'P believes that' should be put at the beginning of condition (3), and, more to the point, the stipulation that (the occurrence of) C is (for Q) a reason *of great weight* (for not doing A) should be omitted. This stipulation, which is loosely-stated enough to fit with any credible evaluative view of coercion (and with the corresponding account of what makes a threat coercive), is not part of what makes something a threat.[48] For that, it suffices that (P believes that) the occurrence of C is for Q a reason, of whatever weight, for not doing A.

The descriptive core of the distinction suffices to reveal its significance for the study of the relationship between threats and normativity. The thought that threats are offensive rested on the notion that to make a threat is to express a willingness to bring about, deliberately, a consequence that the addressee would rather avoid. And when a threat is meant to create a reason to do something that there are other good reasons for doing, the willingness to offend vividly indicates a lack of faith in the addressee's disposition to follow those other reasons—something which itself can be offensive, and which is at odds with the attitude that normally accompanies reliance on the normative method. Now to create a reason *of great weight*, the consequence which a threat involves the communication of a willingness to bring about must be particularly undesirable for the addressee. This would normally make that communication particularly offensive: the willingness to break one's arm is usually more offensive than the willingness to pinch it. And being particularly offensive such a threat, when there are other good reasons for doing what it is meant to prompt the addressee to do, could also be taken to suggest a particularly strong (and hence, again, more offensive) mistrust of the addressee's own judgment.

---

[47] This formulation is a slightly modified version of the one adopted by Raz (above n 6), itself a modification of a formulation offered by Nozick (R Nozick, 'Coercion' in P Laslett, WG Runciman and Q Skinner (eds), *Philosophy, Politics, and Society* (4th series, Oxford, 1972) 104–6).
[48] Similarly the second part of condition (4) deals specifically with the phenomenology of being *coerced* by a threat, rather than that of being issued with a threat in general.

This much is rather trivial, but a stronger point can be made here. To be considered coercive, a threat has to be capable of breaking considerable resistance in the addressee. It usually has to be potentially capable of making the addressee comply no matter to what kind of reasons (if any) her (possible) reluctance to do so may be owed. The actual motivating force of considerations for or against an action may not correspond systematically to distinctions between different classes of reason; but a threat that is only likely to break resistance which is based, for instance, on considerations of convenience, mood, or etiquette, but that seems rather unlikely to make an addressee act against, say, her prudential judgment, moral convictions, or religious beliefs (assuming, that is, that these would counsel against compliance), is unlikely to be considered coercive. Threats which are considered coercive[49] are typically capable, potentially at least, of outweighing all such reasons put together.[50]

The formulation of coercion by threats which I adopted earlier makes no provision for an intention to coerce (or 'coercive intention'). It need not: to be coercive a threat need not be intended as such.[51] In investigating the attitude that typically accompanies the use of coercive threats, however, the observation from the previous paragraph is crucial. The coercive intention is to make the addressee comply no matter how strong her objection, and no matter what reasons for non-compliance she may have or think she has. A coercive threat is thus typically intended, in a sense, to neutralise the addressee's own normative judgment; it is meant to render this judgment, or indeed the very capacity to formulate it, altogether irrelevant for the purposes of determining the addressee's subsequent action. Here we may be reminded that a coercive threat, like any other threat, still requires the addressee to make a choice; and accordingly that the addressee's capacity for normative judgment is still relied upon when such a threat is used. Yet the thrust of the argument remains the same: setting out simply to outweigh every kind of consideration which the addressee could take into

---

[49] This observation (which is, I assume, broad enough to be compatible with every plausible view of the nature of coercion), can be understood as an elaboration of condition (3) in the above formulation of the descriptive core of coercion by threats. Note, however, that it is not implied in condition (4). In circumstances where, for instance, Q has little or no reason to do A, condition (4) may be satisfied even when C is of minor significance, and the threat to bring it about is clearly not coercive.

[50] By allowing that in order to be considered coercive a threat need only *potentially* be capable of outweighing such reasons, the argument is meant to accommodate the notion that a threat may well be considered coercive even when it fails to affect its addressee's behaviour in the desired way (and although the addressee believes that it will be carried out). A certain kind of martyrdom (namely cases where the martyr was given the opportunity to renounce her cause and save her life) provides the most extreme illustration of that possibility. Note, however, that (such) martyrs are the stuff of legend precisely because the threat they chose to defy is of the kind that would normally, or at the very least conceivably, succeed in making a person act against the kind of reason or reasons (moral, religious, etc) on which the martyr acted.

[51] For easy examples of threats which are not intended to be coercive but in fact have such an effect, think of cases where the person issuing the threat is unaware of some particular sensitivity or vulnerability (mental, physical) that the addressee has, and that renders the threatened course of action far more unpleasant or harmful than it would be otherwise.

account in exercising her capacity for normative judgment—indeed, to out-weigh the combined weight of all such considerations—is akin to an attempt to hijack this capacity, rather than genuinely to engage it.[52] And this, as we have seen, is the very same capacity that the use of the normative method can be understood as an invitation to exercise, and on the proper exercise of which it normally depends for its success. The tension between the normative method and the use of coercive threats, in terms of the attitudes that typically accom-pany their use as means of affecting behaviour, thus appears to be particularly acute.

From Threats to Enforceability

The implications of the conclusion arrived at in the previous section must not be exaggerated. The true significance of the incompatibility of the attitudes which typically accompany the use of normativity and the use of threats should be assessed in context, namely when attention is shifted from the somewhat artifi-cial model of an isolated attempt to use both methods at one time, to the exam-ination of the way in which the two may feature in the broader and more dynamic framework of an on-going relationship. Much would depend, of course, on the precise nature of the relationship at stake. Generally speaking, it can be said that the odd use of a threat, and in some cases even a coercive threat, in the framework of a certain relationship need not mean that the related atti-tude dominates or typifies the relationship as a whole, or that this relationship allows no scope for (sincere) normativity or for the attitude which normally accompanies its use.

At this point we should turn to contractual relations. To what extent do the conclusions arrived at thus far apply in this context? Parties to a contract do not, as a matter of course, issue threats to each other. The thought that observations made in and around the discussion of the disjunctive view could have a bearing on the analysis of contractual relations is inspired mostly by the notion that con-tractual obligations are, in principle, enforceable,[53] and that enforceability ful-fils, in the context of the relationship between parties, a similar function to that which threats typically fulfil. As a possible unwelcome consequence attached to a breach (or, at any rate, to contractual behaviour which amounts to harming the other party[54]), enforcement serves as a deterrent to it.[55] By making contracts

---

[52] Compare Raz's account of coercion (by threats and in general) as an invasion of autonomy, above n 6, at 151–57.

[53] In the present context I use 'enforceability' (and, similarly, 'enforcement,' etc) to denote the availability of remedies for breach in general, and not any particular remedy (such as specific per-formance or injunction against breach).

[54] See discussion of remedies in Chapter 4.

[55] To count as an 'unwelcome consequence,' enforcement need not be in the shape of punishment (the common law does not punish breach); it suffices that the defaulting party is made to perform or compensate for non-performance, and is thus deprived of (some of or all) the potential gains from

enforceable, the legal framework provides parties with a special source of reassurance that obligations owed to them will be carried out (or, at least, will not be breached without appropriate redress).[56] In a sense, the legal power to make a contract can be perceived (in part) as the power to have access to and, when necessary, utilise the adjudicating and enforcing mechanisms of the legal system in the pursuit of exchanges with others. Parties to contract could accordingly be described as subjecting each other to the potential deployment of these mechanisms. Moreover, in enforcing contracts, the law—the state—can resort to coercion.[57] This, admittedly, is not usually necessary; but the prospect is well known and is, in fact, precisely what gives the enforceability of contracts its true significance as a deterrent and as a source of reassurance. Thus inasmuch as the analogy between threats and enforceability could be drawn, contractual relations may even appear to be analogous to relations governed by *coercive* threats.[58]

But the analogy is, of course, of but limited application. As far as the observations related to the offensiveness of threats are concerned, it is clearly not sustainable. The availability of remedies for breach is only one possible reason to make a contract (rather than make do, assuming that is possible, with an informal, non-legal arrangement[59]). In certain cultures or sub-cultures or with regard to certain types of agreement, making a formal contract may simply be a

---

the breach (and may be required to cover the plaintiff's legal costs, etc). Also, to have such an effect remedies need not be specifically intended to strip the defendant of her gains (at common law the dominant principle concerning the purpose of remedies is compensating the plaintiff). For discussion and references see Chapter 4.

[56] This is an often commented-upon function of remedies. Economists in particular emphasise the fact that legal enforceability counters uncertainty, thus reducing transaction costs. For a similar emphasis in a somewhat different framework see JL Coleman, *Risks and Wrongs* (Cambridge, 1992) 122–40; and see discussion of remedies in Chapter 4.

[57] The route from a breach of contract to a form of coercive intervention would normally consist of, first, a legal action that may lead to a court order defining a remedial duty; and violation of that order, in turn, may lead to coercive intervention: an award of damages, for example, can be carried to execution, and disobedience of an order of specific performance or of an injunction against breach amounts to contempt of court, and is thus punishable by fine and imprisonment. (See eg GH Treitel, *Remedies for Breach of Contract: A Comparative Account* (Oxford, 1988) 63.)

[58] Note that the notion that enforceability can be a motive for making a contract (rather than a non-legal agreement) does not in any way depend on, nor provide grounds for, the view according to which parties to contracts are (or should be, or should be treated as if they were) indifferent as to whether they will receive performance without litigation or the contract will have to be enforced, or as to whether they will get performance or compensation for non-performance. (For one classic and one contemporary comment on the fallacy of such views see F Pollock, *Principles of Contract* (3rd edn, London, 1881) xix; D Friedmann, 'The Performance Interest in Contract Damages' (1995) 111 *Law Quarterly Review* 628.) The compatibility of this notion with the thought that parties typically have a clear preference for performance without litigation is apparent in light of at least two independent considerations: (1) enforceability can deter a breach in the first place; (2) a party who prefers performance without litigation would still normally wish to have, rather than not have, the option of enforcement in case her first preference is frustrated.

[59] From a legal perspective, there are, in principle, two main channels through which parties to an agreement can willingly avoid legal validity: form (ie by not meeting requirements concerning form where such requirements apply), and intention. See generally GH Treitel, *The Law of Contract* (10th edn, London, 1999) 149–60 (intention) and 161–73 (form); and see my discussion in Chapter 5 of intention to create legal relations.

matter of convention. And even inasmuch as the added confidence afforded by enforceability is known to be a motive—even the main or only motive—to make a contract, the case is clearly still far removed, in terms of the attitudes attributable to the parties and the scope for offence, from one where threats (let alone coercive ones) are explicitly issued.

Earlier we saw that when a threat is used in order to create a reason to do something which there are other (good) reasons for doing, it can be perceived as an indication of a lack of faith, or at any rate a lack of complete or sufficient faith, in the addressee's disposition to follow those other reasons. In this particular sense, the insistence on a contract can, in certain circumstances, be offensive. These circumstances, however, are not typical of contracting. It is mostly in the framework of certain kinds of on-going personal relationship that the desire to enjoy the added reassurance that a legally binding contract can provide would be at odds with the kind of mutual trust which the parties can reasonably expect to enjoy, so that, as Atiyah put it, 'to try to invoke formal contract . . . often destroys the very trust on which the relationship is based.'[60] When dealing with a stranger, by contrast, such a desire would not normally seem out of place and should not normally offend. And in contrast to the case of promises, on-going personal relationships are by no means the paradigmatic framework for making contracts.

Yet other observations made in the course of discussing the disjunctive view are readily applicable to the analysis of contractual relations and their comparison to promissory ones. In the next chapter I will examine the comparable effect that the enforceability of contracts has on the role designated for trust, and on the scope that is left for 'expressive reasons' in the contractual framework. These themes are particularly significant for the comparison of contract to promise: both, as I will argue, concern qualities that set contracts apart from their non-legal equivalents.

---

[60] *Essays On Contract* (Oxford, 1986) Essay 4: 'Fuller and the Theory of Contract' at 78. Atiyah refers here, approvingly, to an observation made by Fuller in *The Principles of Social Order* (Durham, North Carolina, 1981) 185: 'Within the close-knit family, demands for a contractual spelling out of obligations will seem to imply an inappropriate distrust.' Note that the same can sometimes be true even of promises: a demand for an explicit promise ('I want you *to promise me* that you'll do that') can be at odds with the kind of trust or confidence the addressee expects to be enjoying already in the context in which it is made. This is likely to be the case, however, in a more limited range of relationships compared to that in which the invocation of formal contract is likely to offend—closer or more intimate relationships, relationships in the context of which more can be expected to go without saying, etc.

3

The Nature and Value of
Contractual Relations

H AVING EXAMINED, AND largely rejected, the 'disjunctive' view, the stage is
set, back in the context of comparing contract to promise, for the introduction of a more moderate thesis: a thesis according to which the two simply
differ. The first part of this chapter examines differences in terms of the way in
which contract and promise fulfil their similar instrumental function. Drawing
directly on previous discussions, it focuses on the relationship between the
enforceability of contracts and the role reserved for trust in the practice. While
the argument of the second part of the chapter could be viewed as the other side
of the same coin, its conclusions are likely to be farther reaching still. The focus
here is on the intrinsic functions attributable to contract and to promise, and the
very notion that these are similar will come under scrutiny.

I. CONTRACTS AND THE ROLE OF TRUST

Enforceability and the Trivialisation of the Role of Trust

Typically enforceable as they are, contracts provide parties with a special source
of reassurance that obligations owed to them will be discharged.[1] The availability of remedies need not be thought of merely as a safety net for those who
were harmed (or are about to be harmed) as a consequence of a breach: by dra-
matically decreasing the likelihood that a defaulting party would benefit
through harming the other party, it functions (or, at any rate, *should* function[2])
as a deterrent to conduct that amounts to causing such harm. At this point we
may be reminded that the act of promising can sometimes give rise to reasons to
keep the promise—and, accordingly, reasons to believe that the promise will be
kept—that do not directly reflect whatever it is that justifies the requirement
to keep a promise in the first place, and, more to the point, seem to play a role

---

[1] Whether, in the context of a given legal system, these are understood to be obligations to perform, or to compensate for non-performance, etc. See also below n 38.
[2] See discussion of remedies in Chapter 4.

similar to that which the enforceability of contract plays in these respects. A promisor may, for example, be discouraged from breaking her promise by the prospect of a loss of reputation or of facing some hostile reactions, while the promisee, aware of this background, may gain reassurance (that the promise will be kept) through a similar channel.[3] Yet the difference is clear. Enforceability is built into contract in a way that no equivalent source of reassurance is built into promise. Unlike the possible adverse effects of a broken promise, the legal aftermath of an unjustified breach is not speculative and contingent but known and, for the most part, certain. And, significantly, it is administered by purposely designed and famously powerful institutionalised mechanisms—mechanisms which are unique to the legal system.[4]

But what implications does that have in terms of trust? It is perhaps tempting to think of the enforceability of contract as an alternative to trust; to think that while in promise trust is required, as a normal background condition, in order for the practice to function properly, enforceability simply does away with this requirement. But there is something misleading about this suggestion, for in contract, too, a certain kind of trust is usually necessary. Especially in light of the typical preference for performance without litigation, it could be surmised that parties to contract have to trust their counterparts *to keep the contract*. How is that different from the role trust plays in promise?

Bearing in mind that trust, like reassurance, doubt or suspicion, can be a matter of degree, it could first be suggested, as a sensible modification of the original proposition, that enforceability enables parties to have sufficient confidence while trusting their counterparts *less* than they would normally have to without it; in other words that trusting a person to keep a contract simply requires less trust compared to trusting a person to keep a (non-legal) promise. Yet there is a more illuminating way in which to characterise, perhaps in addition, the difference between contract and promise in terms of the role trust is called upon to play in each of the practices. It could be described as a difference in terms of the sense in which participants in the two practices normally have to trust their counterparts. The transition from promise to contract can, in this respect, be characterised as marking a shift from the kind of trust that is likely to obtain mostly in the framework of (certain kinds of) pre-existing personal relationships, to trust in a more trivial sense—the kind of trust that is likely to obtain (even) between strangers. Let me explain, starting with a few general observations about the concept of trust.

---

[3] Of course such reasons need not, and normally would not, be entirely unrelated to what justifies or requires in the first place the action for which they are reasons. At least, normally they reflect the fact that such a justification exists, or is believed to exist: hostile reactions or a loss of reputation typically occur precisely because breaking a promise is believed to be wrong, and it is believed to be wrong for a reason. See discussion in Chapter 1, and later in this chapter.

[4] For a similar point see TM Scanlon, 'Promises and Contracts' in P Benson (ed), *The Theory of Contract: New Essays* (Cambridge, 2001) 86, at 99.

'To trust a person' (or a thing) is a highly context-sensitive concept. In utterances such as 'I trust the weather will be nice tomorrow,' 'trust' stands for, roughly, a combination of a belief (more or less firm), and a welcoming or approving attitude towards the subject of the belief.[5] These two elements are present in expressions of trust in a person: to trust a person is to believe that she possesses some favourable attribute. But the content and significance of an expression of trust in a person—the nature and the weight of the attribute in question—may vary considerably from one context to another. It may be a character trait, a capacity, or a skill; it may be something that the person has permanently or temporarily; it may range in significance from the trivial to the profound. In the context of recruiting accomplices for a bank robbery, for instance, 'I trust her' may be an expression of faith in someone's expertise with explosives; in the context of deciding who should drive on the way back from the pub, 'I trust Kimi' may reflect no more than the belief that Kimi is a reasonably good driver, and that he is not quite as drunk as the rest of us; yet in other contexts, expressions of trust are intended as weighty, sweeping statements about a person's character or moral worth.

Thus far in this work, 'trust' has featured in the context of two different discussions: that concerning the employment of the normative method, and that concerning participation in the practice of making promises. The typical implications of its invocation in both are similar. In both contexts, to begin with, trust has to do with people's (those in whom trust is expressed) responsiveness to practical reasons.[6] Admittedly, this need not amount to much: the capacity and disposition to respond correctly to certain reasons is something that is commonly taken more or less for granted, and, as such, rarely gives rise to expressions of trust at all.[7] Think, for instance, of practical decisions that require no more than the application of rather obvious 'means to an end' logic, or, where there is a choice to be made, involve forming (or displaying) an order of priorities which could hardly be disputed or confused. Such cases may roughly be described as ones where people exercise, and display, (no more than) basic rationality; and in normal circumstances, having a belief in a person's basic rationality and no more could at best be described as a rather trivial sense in which to trust (a sane adult, at any rate). Yet promises (typically) and the normative method (often[8]) involve trust in a much more profound sense. For a start, a correct response to the reasons to which people are expected to respond in these contexts (the promise, a command, etc) usually requires a degree of

---

[5] Utterances such as 'I trust the weather will be nasty tomorrow' (when nasty weather is not a welcome proposition) are of course acceptable, but in such cases 'trust' is usually used in a sarcastic or humorous way.

[6] The term 'responsiveness' is used here in a broad sense. It may involve, inter alia and according to circumstances, identifying a reason, weighing it (possibly against competing reasons), ascribing to it the correct exclusionary force, and following it.

[7] See eg Chapter 2 on threats and trust.

[8] See *ibid*.

sophistication and abstraction that clearly transcends what I labelled as basic rationality. More importantly, trusting a person to keep a promise[9] (and, in many cases, to follow the reasons for action created when the normative method is employed) usually amounts to seeing her in a certain favourable moral light. Whether the attitude in question is described (in the case of promises) as seeing the promisor as the kind of person who stands by her word, or who treats others with respect or is generally honest, the implications are typically in terms of the promisor's moral worth, of her possessing some character trait which, in this particular respect, renders her a good, moral person. In Chapter 1 we encountered the claim that to say 'I promise to be there' is tantamount to saying, 'I'll be there. Trust me.'[10] Clearly this rings true only inasmuch as the promisor, rather than merely declaring herself in possession of basic rationality, is understood to allude to trust in this far from trivial, moral sense.

This kind of trust cannot be expected generally to obtain between strangers. And contracts, unlike promises, are habitually made outside the framework of on-going personal relationships. The contractual framework, however, makes it manifestly unlikely (or less likely) that a party would benefit from illegitimately harming her counterpart through a breach. And as a reason to refrain from such conduct, enforceability, like the typical threat, does not so much hinge on the parties' goodwill, decency, or moral character in general. It renders the keeping of a contract (or, at any rate, refraining from conduct that amounts to illegitimately harming the other party) largely a matter of basic rationality, and, accordingly, renders the belief in the other party's basic rationality a sufficient basis on which to trust it to keep the contract (or, at any rate, to behave as expected upon entering the contract). Trust in this rather trivial sense thus replaces, as a normal requirement, the kind of trust—trust in a rather profound, moral sense—that normally features in the promissory context.

To be sure, the point made here is not that personal trust in its non-trivial (or less trivial) sense is somehow *excluded* from contractual relations (the 'disjunctive view' has been rejected!), nor that in the framework of contractual relations it is rendered wholly irrelevant: normally it would be most desirable, if only for the fact that no matter how confident parties may be even without it, an extra source of reassurance should still count as a welcome bonus. The point is merely that the legal framework enables parties to have sufficient reassurance even in circumstances of considerable ignorance as to the personal attributes of their counterparts—circumstances in which trust in its more profound sense is less likely to obtain, and which are, crucially, rather common for contracting.

[9] More accurately, trusting the promisor to break the promise if and only if it would be justified to do so (the 'correct response' to a promise is to keep it *other things being equal*).
[10] The claim is by Scanlon. See Chapter 1, n 23 at 211.

Trust and the True Nature of the Practice

A further point can be introduced through the re-examination of a line of criticism that could be directed against the argument thus far, and that has already arisen in the course of presenting it.

The criticism in question is that there may be something arbitrary in highlighting the significance of the role of personal trust in promise and its trivialisation in contract; that the way in which these practices function in reality tells a somewhat different story. For in the contexts of both, reasons for action (to keep a promise, to abide by the terms of a contract) and reasons for belief (that promissory or contractual obligations will be discharged) of various types can often be found at work, and an equivalent of the feature which has been described as the hallmark of one practice can in fact be identified as operative in the other, too, and vice versa. Thus in promise, and particularly where the practice is fairly well-established, hostile reactions (from the promisee or others), loss of reputation, and the like, are prospects that frequently await a promisor who unjustifiably reneges on her promise, making it manifestly unlikely that she will be better off as a result. This, in turn, may well give rise both to reasons to keep the promise and to the belief that the promise will be kept; and the kind of trust that hinges upon such a belief (in such circumstances) need not be qualitatively different, more profound, than the kind of 'trivial' personal trust that has been described as a distinct possibility in the context of trusting a person to keep a contract. At the same time in contract, the kind of personal trust that is less trivial, the kind that is related to a belief in a person's moral worth and not merely basic rationality, is not only, as I mentioned earlier, typically considered most welcome, but is not too rarely deemed indispensable. People sometimes explain a reluctance to enter contractual relations by saying things like, 'I don't trust this person.' And while such utterances are not usually perceived as reflecting some conceptual confusion concerning contract, the mistrust they express need not be to the effect that the person in question is straightforwardly irrational, or that she is likely to break the contract and then escape jurisdiction.

In reply to this line of criticism I would insist that, despite this duality, the contrasting features which were highlighted in connection with each practice—the role reserved for (non-trivial) personal trust in promise, enforceability as a source of reassurance and the trivialisation of the role of trust in contract—are indicative of the true nature of that practice but not the other. The idea, in other words, is that the presence of these features in one practice is somehow less contingent and more significant than the presence of similar features in the other. This line of thought was introduced briefly earlier, along with the line of criticism to which it serves as a reply; but here I wish to offer a slightly more nuanced argument in its support.

It should be a useful strategy to focus on the way in which (the equivalent of) the attribute that was described as characteristic of one practice features in the other, and vice versa. Now the main point concerning promises has already been mentioned. It is that the adverse aftermath of a breach, as well as its exact nature (loss of reputation, hostile reactions, etc) and intensity, is, essentially, a contingency. In certain contexts it may be more probable, and as a source of reasons (to keep a promise, to believe it will be kept) more powerful than in others. But the practice in general does not provide for such an aftermath on any systematic basis, and can hardly be understood as designed to make participants respond to its probability. This combines with the fact that as a matter of explaining the normative foundations of the practice, the prospect of hostile reactions to a breach of promise (or similarly adverse effects thereof) is merely indicative of the fact that participants are expected to act for some other, unrelated, reason or reasons—an expectation that could explain or justify such hostile reactions but that cannot be explained by them. The possibility of hostile reactions, in other words, must be logically secondary to something that could independently justify, or at least widely be thought to justify, the proposition that promises ought to be kept in the first place, and with it justify and motivate such reactions to a failure to do so.

The combined force of these mutually-reinforcing considerations is to show that the prospect of hostile reactions (and the like), as well the kind of reasons or motives to which it is likely to give rise and the kind of trust which hinges upon such reasons, all play but a limited role in explaining the rationale of the practice and in shaping its normal mode of operation. Now in contract enforceability could be described as logically secondary in a similar way: after all it, too, reflects the logically prior notion that contractual undertakings ought to be performed (or that non-performance or the loss it entails should be compensated for, etc). But the remedial aspect of contract is integrated into the practice in a way that renders this consideration, at least as far as the participants are concerned, largely irrelevant. The precise rules, procedures, and mechanisms of remedies are all part and parcel of the practice's formal, institutional structure. Indeed the remedial aspect of contracts is so much an integral part of the practice, and so much of a predominant part at that, as to have led some to adopt the exaggerated view according to which the practice as a whole is *all about* remedies, or that the core contractual obligation is not at all an obligation to perform but rather the essentially remedial obligation to compensate for non-performance.[11]

A further point, while related to and capable of further establishing the argument thus far, is farther reaching still. It is that, in stark contrast to the case of promise, where, as we saw, the role personal trust in its non-trivial sense plays in the practice reflects the practice's very rationale and underlies its proper mode of operation, the equivalent role that (non-trivial) personal trust is called upon

---

[11] The classic exponent of such a view is Holmes. See OW Holmes, *The Common Law* (Boston, 1881), eg at 300–1; PS Atiyah, *Essays on Contract* (Oxford, 1986), Essay 3: 'Holmes and the Theory of Contract'; and see discussion of remedies in Chapter 4.

to play in contract is owed, in large part at least, to factors which could only be described as pervasive *defects* in the functioning of legal systems. This point can be born out through a comparison of legal reality to a model of an ideally functioning practice.

In his 'Essays on the Nature of Contracts,' Ian Macneil compiled a list of the various limitations involved in legal remedies for breach of contract.[12] Conceding that the legal devices available to a (potential) plaintiff may 'add to the assurance' that 'the promise will be fulfilled,' Macneil went on to illustrate why not 'even ironclad legal rights of enforcement' provide complete certainty, and that in fact 'countless obstacles lie between [statements of positive law that ostensibly guarantee performance or its equivalent] and what is practically available to an injured party through legal process.'[13] Chief amongst those obstacles and limitations are the fact that the remedies awarded are not always the ones that best protect the plaintiff's interest, the transaction costs and other burdens involved in resorting to the legal process, and finally, even after winning the 'right' judgment, the potential difficulties involved in enforcing it.[14] All true, of course. Now in a different, broader context—that of studying political authorities—Joseph Raz observed the following:

> Reality has a way of falling short of the ideal. . . . [N]aturally not even legitimate authorities always succeed, nor do they always try to live up to the ideal. It is nevertheless through their ideal functioning that they must be understood. For that is how they are supposed to function, that is how they publicly claim that they attempt to function, . . . and naturally authorities are judged and their performance evaluated by comparing them to the ideal.[15]

With this in mind, let us proceed on the basic assumption that, as Daniel Friedmann wrote, '[t]he essence of contract is performance'[16]; and that accordingly, the role designated for remedies is, first and foremost, to protect what is known in the literature as 'the performance interest.'[17] As I mentioned earlier, remedies can potentially fulfil this role not only when actually awarded, but also by serving as a deterrent to conduct that amounts to (illegitimately)

---

[12] (1980) 10 *Southern Carolina Central Law Journal* 159. Extracts from this article were reprinted in D Campbell (ed), *The Relational Theory of Contract: Selected Works of Ian Macneil* (London, 2001) (henceforth: *Macneil, Selected Works*). For similar observations see also H Collins, *Regulating Contracts* (Oxford, 1999) 101, 269–70.

[13] *Macneil, Selected Works*, at 266.

[14] *Ibid* at 266–67. Note that, having listed these limitations, Macneil went on to explain why they 'do not, however, erode our overall contract system as much as one might think.' Amongst the considerations he listed to explain this is the availability of various 'supporting' legal devices, such as allowance to claim the costs of litigation back from the defendant, provisions allowing class action, etc. See *ibid* at 267–68.

[15] *The Morality of Freedom* (Oxford, 1986) 47.

[16] 'The Performance Interest in Contract Damages' (1995) 111 *Law Quarterly Review* 628, at 629.

[17] See *ibid*. This assumption is investigated in Chapter 4. Note, however, that the argument to follow does not depend for its validity on the truth of this assumption: it would apply, *mutatis mutandis*, if the core contractual obligation were, for instance, compensation for loss in reliance, and the main role assigned to remedies were the protection of the reliance interest.

undermining the interest they protect. Now imagine a legal system where obtaining a remedy for a breach is, for the innocent party, cost-free, quick, and mostly trouble-free. Moreover, the remedy awarded is always the right one— always the remedy that, in the circumstances, best reflects concern for the performance interest and best protects it.[18] And, to complete the picture, in cases where remedial duties are not performed promptly, they are enforced effectively, and in a similar fashion: quickly, cost-free, trouble-free. The point to be made here is simple: the closer a legal system is to perfection in such respects, the more likely and more apparent it becomes that a defaulting party will, if anything, be worse off as a result of defaulting. Consequently, discharging contractual obligations (or, at any rate, refraining from an unjustified breach, or from conduct that amounts to illegitimately harming the other party) in such a system would be more a matter of basic rationality, and contractual confidence would be less dependent upon trust in anything beyond the sense which corresponds to a belief in a person's possession of the capacity for basic rationality.

Of course even against the background of an ideally functioning practice there is no reason to think that, *given the choice*, people would not prefer to make contracts with others whom they happen to trust more (or in a deeper, less trivial sense) rather than less: they probably would, if only because it is nicer to do things in a more amicable way, let alone that, as noted earlier, no matter how confident they may feel regardless, an extra source of confidence should still be welcome. The crucial point, however, is that an ideally functioning practice would generally enable people to make contracts and have sufficient reassurance even when no such choice exists. Similarly it would be wrong to assume that against the background of an ideally functioning practice the typical preference for performance without litigation would no longer obtain. (Although such a background may well have the side effect of denying this preference some of its intensity: after all, some major reasons for dreading litigation are removed.) Rather, the point is that in an ideally functioning practice, parties who do prefer performance without litigation would feel particularly confident, largely regardless of whether or not they trust their counterparts in all but a trivial sense, that this very preference will be satisfied. And, returning from the ideal to reality, the point is that inasmuch as in reality contractual confidence depends upon non-trivial trust to a greater extent than in the ideal, this is as indicative of the true nature of the practice, as indicative of the practice's true purpose and proper mode of operation, as are factors such as the spiralling cost and slow pace of litigation, the occasional adoption by legal institutions of wrong policies or rules, or judicial mistakes.

---

[18] For a concise taxonomy of contract remedies and their relationship to the performance interest, see above n 16, 629–32; and see discussion of remedies in Chapter 4.

Preview

Viewed in isolation, the discussion thus far in this chapter may seem to fall short of establishing that there is a significant difference between the legal and the non-legal practices under examination. It may be thought, for instance, that the emerging conclusion is that the legal practice is no more than an improved version of its non-legal equivalent, for it facilitates a similar pursuit while simply alleviating a burden—that of dependence on trust—that afflicts the normal operation of promise. Such a conclusion, however, would be wide of the mark. To see the role trust plays in promise as nothing but a burden is to see but one side of the coin, and not necessarily the more important side; whilst the notion that the enforceability of contract has no implications beyond the alleviation of such a burden is an oversight of similar magnitude. Both these propositions have emerged already in Chapter 1 and Chapter 2. In the rest of this chapter they will be further investigated, and their implications for the comparison between contract and promise explained.

II. CONTRACTS, PROMISES AND SPECIAL RELATIONS

The discussion in the first part of this chapter focused on how promise and contract fulfil a similar function—one which, in the earlier discussion of promises, I labelled as the practice's 'instrumental' function: facilitating a form of reliance, co-operation, or co-ordination between people. The differences I described, in terms of the way in which the two practices fulfil this function, can be viewed as both an indication and a result of dissimilarity in terms of the circumstances in which promises and contracts are normally called upon to fulfil this function: whereas promises are normally made in the framework of some on-going personal relationship, with the case of promises between strangers accounted for as the exception,[19] in the case of contract the opposite is true: the practice as a whole is designed, first and foremost, to facilitate co-operation or mutual reliance between strangers, while making do with the kind of trust that is likely to obtain between strangers (so that the invocation of the practice in the context of personal relations can sometimes be utterly inappropriate[20]). Still despite these differences, the instrumental function each of the practices fulfils remains by and large the same function, and the principal method by which it fulfils it— providing a framework for and regulating (some of) the normative consequences of voluntary undertakings of obligations to others—essentially the same method.

---

[19] See Chapter 1 on promises between strangers.
[20] See Chapter 2, from threats to enforceability.

In the discussion of promises, however, it was argued that this practice potentially fulfils yet another function, and may accordingly be understood to possess
yet another value. Labelled as the 'intrinsic value' of the practice, it has to do
with (as Raz put it) 'the desirability of special bonds between people and the
desirability of special relations that are voluntarily shaped and developed by the
choice of participants.'[21] Does the similarity of function and value between contract and promise continue here, too? As I indicated earlier, I will answer this
question in the negative, arguing that contract, as a practice, cannot be understood as designed to promote special relations or special bonds the way the practice of promise does.

This view may appear, at first glance, to be an inevitable, and at that rather
obvious, implication of facts which have been established already in the course
of previous discussions. For we have seen that, in contrast to promise, the practice of contract can be understood as designed to function specifically in the
absence of pre-existing relations between parties. Does not this claim alone give
the game away? I do not think that it does. Contracts may indeed not depend,
in the sense which promises typically do, on pre-existing relations, and may typically be made between strangers; yet once a contract is made, a relationship
of sorts is invariably established between its parties. And there is no obvious
reason for thinking that this kind of relationship is in any way less valuable
than promissory relations typically are. Perhaps, even, contracts only excel here:
perhaps they promote special relations even where promises cannot or are
unlikely to do so.

We clearly need a better understanding of the concept of special relations as
it features in the present discussion.

What is Special in Special Relations?

'Special relations' may be taken to denote a situation where people owe duties
to each other that they do not owe to others (or, at any rate, do not owe to
people in general).[22] Such duties are usually referred to in the literature as 'special duties' or 'special obligations.' On this understanding of special relations,
the problem of comparing contracts and promises in terms of the extent to
which they derive value from 'the desirability of special relations' receives an

---

[21] J Raz, 'Book Review: Promises in Morality and Law' (1982) 95 *Harvard Law Review* 916, at
928.

[22] Raz's account of the binding force of promises can be understood as capturing this sense of
special relations: '[The principles stating when promises are binding] present promises as creating a
relation between the promisor and promisee—which is taken out of the general competition of conflicting reasons. It creates a special bond, binding the promisor to be, in the matter of the promise,
partial to the promisee. It obliges the promisor to regard the claims of the promisee as not just one
of the many claims that every person has for his respect and help but as having peremptory force.'
('Promises and Obligations' in P Hacker and J Raz (eds), *Law, Morality and Society* (Oxford, 1977)
227–28.)

instant answer, and not the one I hinted at the outset. Promise and contract both involve the voluntary creation of individually-owed obligations. And if this is all there is to special relations, then it would seem that promises and contracts promote special relations in the same way and probably to the same extent. If anything, on this understanding contracts would appear to be more conducive to special relations than promises, for a contract normally involves a bilateral undertaking of special obligations whereas a promise is, essentially, a unilateral undertaking,[23] let alone that (as we have seen) contracts facilitate the undertaking of special obligations outside (or, at any rate, not only inside) the framework of already-existing relationships, and therefore in a wider range of circumstances than promises.

Some think that special obligations are an indispensable feature of any meaningful form of human relationship.[24] I will not want to argue against this view. But I do wish to suggest that the concept of 'special relations' need not, for present purposes, be understood to entail or involve nothing other than the existence of such obligations. To that end let me start with a few general observations, intended as entirely uncontroversial, concerning personal relationships.[25]

First, still concerning special obligations, it should be useful to bear in mind that there is more than one way in which these may relate to a given relationship, or indeed more than one way in which the two concepts—special relations, special obligations—may be linked. A relationship (special or otherwise) may simply *be* a set of individually-owed obligations (that is, the very fact that certain obligations are owed, and owed individually, may be said to constitute a special relationship between the individuals involved), but a relationship may also be capable of *generating* special obligations (and perhaps in this sense be considered special).[26] A contract, to illustrate the distinction, typically designates a set of obligations that its parties owe each other. In this very sense, a contract may be said to create a relationship between the parties—a relationship that is defined, and the meaning of which is exhausted by this very set of obligations. It would of course be misleading to suggest that a contract merely creates a relationship, and that contractual obligations, in turn, are created by or flow from this relationship. It is, however, a separate, and a far more contentious question, as to whether or to what extent contractual relations can

---

[23] This point will be resumed and refined in the next section.

[24] '[W]e would be hard pressed to find any type of human relationship to which people have attached value or significance but which has never been seen as generating [special] responsibilities. It seems that whenever people value an interpersonal relationship they are apt to see it as a source of special duties or obligations': S Scheffler, *Boundaries and Allegiances: Problems of Justice and Responsibility in Liberal Thought* (Oxford, 2001), 98.

[25] None of the points to be made in what follows are intended as linguistic ones. As far as linguistic points are concerned, however, it is perhaps tempting to suggest that if the occurrence of special obligations is indeed a standard feature of human relationships in general, it could hardly count as what makes certain relationships special.

[26] Scheffler's quotation, above n 24, clearly alludes to the latter possibility.

generate obligations over and above, or in place of, those created directly by the contract.[27]

More importantly, there are aspects of personal relationships that go beyond special obligations altogether, and this remains true no matter what type of link between special obligations and special relations we have in mind. To highlight this fact, let me add two more observations. First, what parties to a relationship owe each other as parties to a relationship need not always amount to obligations (and perhaps 'owe' is, accordingly, too strong a term to use here). Relationships often comprise various standards of conduct, and standards that vary, among other things, in terms of their deontic status. As a friend, for instance, one may have various obligations to one's friends, but friendship can also entail that it would be *advisable* to do certain things, that it would be *nice* or merely alright to do or to refrain from doing other things, and so on. If we take the word 'responsibility' to encompass this variety, then it could be said that relationships often involve individually-owed (or 'special') responsibilities, possibly some of which in the form of obligations, and some in other, deontically milder forms.

Finally, consider the following questions. Suppose it could be possible to articulate the full network of individually-owed obligations and other special responsibilities that some personal relationship entails. Is it always clear that the ensuing list captures the full meaning, significance, and value that the relationship holds or may hold for its parties? And what if some of these responsibilities are not fulfilled: would that inevitably mean that the relationship is less valuable for the parties? Would the reduction necessarily be by a similar proportion to that of the unfulfilled, or perhaps unacknowledged, responsibilities? If none are acknowledged, would that invariably mean that the relationship lacks significance altogether? If all are discharged, would that mean that the relationship could not possibly be tightened, deepened, made more valuable still?

It is tempting to say that the more profound the type of inter-personal relationship with regard to which such questions are posed, the clearer it becomes that they should all be answered in the negative; or to say that a relationship deserves to be called 'special' precisely for comprising valuable elements that are not reducible to the list of special responsibilities that it involves. It could safely be stated, at any rate, that personal relationships are often like this. Relationships are often valuable for their parties over and above, and sometimes altogether regardless of, the value the parties place on the responsibilities individually owed to them in or as a result of the relationship. Special responsibilities, to put it simply, are by no means the only building blocks of which personal relationships are constructed, and by no means the only source of

---

[27] This issue arises particularly in connection with the category known as 'relational contracts.' Problems pertaining specifically to this category deserve a separate discussion that cannot be pursued here, but I will comment on it briefly later in this chapter (see below on personal detachment and relational contract) and in Chapter 5 on freedom from contract.

meaning, significance, and value of the kind that personal relationships often hold.

What are, then, those additional building blocks? It would, I think, be silly to try and list in the abstract all the possible elements that make relationships significant or meaningful, or that endow them with the particular value they hold for their parties. At the very least, it could be pointed out that it is usually the case that the meaning, significance, and value of a personal relationship for its parties cannot be separated from the fact that it is a relationship with the very person it is a relationship with (is this not the main sense in which a relationship can be said to be 'personal'?)—and all the attributes which in any meaningful way make a person the person she is (or, rather, the person she appears to be to others) potentially come into this. Also (inasmuch as this is distinct from character or appearance of character in general), usually crucial in personal relationships are the parties' attitudes (or what appear to be their attitudes) towards each other, with everything, all the feelings, intentions, hopes, misgivings, that can come into that.

Let us narrow the scope and focus on the latter. Clearly, the meaning and significance of people's attitudes towards others with whom they have personal relationships normally cannot be entirely reduced to or explained away in terms of their special responsibilities, or, for that matter, the things they do or have to do for each other or with regard to each other, or their actions in general. Yet this does not mean that there is no connection between such attitudes and special responsibilities. For one thing, as constitutive elements in what gives personal relationships their meaning, significance, and value, parties' attitudes toward each other presumably have some role to play in explaining how relationships generate special responsibilities (inasmuch as they do). And more importantly for present purposes, it is through actions which are taken in the context of a relationship that such attitudes are habitually expressed or revealed.

Indeed, many things people do as parties to a relationship matter particularly for the range of attitudes which are expressed, intentionally or not, through them. Actions taken in discharging special responsibilities are no exception. Such actions often assume significance and value over and above their immediate instrumental value as the actions they are, and over and above, if not wholly regardless of, the value they may derive specifically from being actions by which responsibilities are discharged. They do this precisely through being a medium for conveying attitudes which are themselves pivotal building blocks of personal relationships, often no less pivotal, and sometimes much more so, than the special responsibilities which a relationship may involve, or the recognition of these responsibilities as such by the parties.

More than just a possibility, the expressive quality of actions taken in discharging special responsibilities reflects something that goes to the heart of most types of personal relationship, and that informs and greatly complicates much of the expectations that parties to such relationships typically have and typically face. Friends, for example, are generally expected to be aware of the special obligations they have as friends; but at the same time when discharging their special obligations, friends are usually expected not to be (or appear to be) too aware, so to speak, of the fact that these are obligations. A person who promptly discharges all the special obligations she has as a friend, but discharges them mostly out of a sense of duty (or, at any rate, so that this appears to be the case) is unlikely to be considered a good friend. Admittedly, 'sense of duty' is somewhat ambiguous in this context. If it reflects an understanding as to why the actions at stake are obligatory or how such obligations emanate from the relationship, such an understanding may itself count in her favour and render her capable of friendship or even of being a reasonably good friend, if not much more. But think of a person who only recognises and discharges her special obligations thanks to *The Comprehensive Guide to Friendship*, a publication that lists all the possible obligations (and other responsibilities) one owes to one's friends and all the possible circumstances in which these obligations arise, together with their precise implications in every such case. Whatever her motives to follow the guide and however accurately she does so, it seems very doubtful that such a person could be described as a real friend at all, let alone a good one (or, for that matter, doubtful that *The Comprehensive Guide to Friendship* is worthy of its title[28]).

Yet not all relationships are like this. A certain pre-condition needs to be satisfied in order for a relationship to form a framework within which actions habitually derive special value from the attitudes they serve to convey, and to be a framework which is thus valuable in itself in a special way. This pre-condition has to do with transparency. In order for parties to be able to express their attitudes towards their counterparts in discharging their special responsibilities, and in order for them to be able to discern significance and value in actions taken in discharging special responsibilities owed to them, the setting must allow for a certain measure of transparency—of the relevant attitudes, or of the motives for the actions through which attitudes manifest themselves. Now motives are almost never entirely transparent. More often than not they are mixed and multi-layered; and people's precise motives are often somewhat obscure to themselves, let alone others. Yet in the context of many types of personal relationship, people habitually ascribe motives and attitudes to their counterparts, and do so with a reasonable degree of success. People may rarely be entirely transparent in their behaviour, but they are equally rarely entirely opaque, at least as far as their friends, lovers, close colleagues, family members and the like are concerned. And it is the transparency (or, at any rate, the illusion of transparency), however imperfect or incomplete, that such relationships typically afford that enables them to be an arena in which actions can relatively

---

[28] Although a person's motives to follow *The Comprehensive Guide to Friendship* may well be relevant in assessing her personality in general, or in assessing exactly how incapable of friendship she might be.

easily assume an expressive content that makes them significant and valuable in ways they would not otherwise be.

It would be correct to point out in response that when actions taken in the context of a relationship assume special significance as manifestations of certain attitudes, the relationship is valuable, first and foremost, for the fact that its parties have these attitudes, and not for the fact that it provides a framework in which such attitudes can manifest themselves through certain actions. Indeed, since it is almost tautological to say that in order for a relationship to be valuable for its parties for (inter alia) the kind of inter-personal attitudes involved, the parties need to have a sense of what these attitudes are, it is also clear that the pre-condition of transparency needs to be satisfied simply in order for a relationship to be valuable in this way, and not specifically in order for the relevant attitudes to be manifested through the discharging of special responsibilities.[29] The emphasis I have placed here on the way and the conditions under which such actions can enhance the value of personal relations, however, derives from our ultimate interest in certain special obligations (promissory, contractual) and their respective roles in shaping the relationships in the context of which they are undertaken and performed. Let us now concentrate on those.

Thus far I have not distinguished, in terms of their respective (expressive-content related) contributions to the value of relationships, between actions that are directly related to special obligations, and other actions that may be taken in the context of a relationship but that have little to do with such obligations, or indeed with special responsibilities in general. Two considerations need be mentioned in this context, in correlation with the two principal ways in which actions can relate to special obligations. Actions by which special obligations (or other special responsibilities) are *discharged* are particularly suitable for manifesting those attitudes that the parties have towards each other, but not

---

[29] Relationships arising out of membership are a typical example of a case where the attitudes that give the relationship (much of) its meaning and value are not usually manifested through actions taken on its inter-personal front. In his discussion of the subject, Samuel Scheffler maintained that if a person values her membership in a 'socially recognized group,' she is likely to value her relationships with fellow members of the same group. ('[T]wo members of a socially recognized group do have a relationship . . . even if they have never met, and if they value their membership in that group they may also value their relations to the other members': above n 24, at 102.) To my mind this view should be treated with caution: I may value my membership in, say, an ethnic or a national group for a variety of reasons, yet not see myself as having valuable personal relations, or indeed as having any kind of personal relations, with fellow members as such. Scheffler's view seems plausible only inasmuch as the group at stake is such that membership in it can reasonably clearly indicate what it is that makes it valuable for members to be members, so that such shared attitudes could serve as a basis on which members may consider themselves as having some meaningful form of relationship despite the absence of any form of interactivity. For this, it would normally have to be the case that membership is voluntary (otherwise, what ostensible indication is there that members *value* their membership at all?), and the range of reasons for valuing it fairly limited (the less diverse the reasons, the less equivocal the indication). This is mainly why membership in a national group provides a rather inadequate illustration for Scheffler's argument: such memberships are largely non-voluntary, and the reasons (if any) for valuing them multitudinous and highly diverse: the requisite transparency, in other words, does not obtain.

necessarily towards other people (after all special obligations are, by definition, individually owed). Then there are those actions by which special obligations are *undertaken*. Especially when such actions are voluntary and intentional, the undertaking itself can sometimes manifest attitudes which are highly significant in the context of personal relations. Since contracts and promises both involve special obligations which are (typically) undertaken intentionally and voluntarily, both sides of the distinction will have to be looked at when, in the next section, contracts and promises will be compared in terms of their respective roles in creating and enhancing special relations.

Contracts, Promises and Special Relations

Let me clarify from the outset that I am not going to deny that something similar to a possibility identified in passing with regard to memberships can occur both in contract and in promise.[30] The possibility is that a person would place value on a contract she is a party to or on a promise given to her, without seeing herself as having any meaningful form of personal relations or any kind of personal bond with the other party to the contract or with the promisor—at least not a relationship the meaning and value of which could not be entirely reduced to or explained in terms of the special obligations (contractual or promissory) involved, or the value of these obligations for those to whom they are owed.[31] At the same time, I am not going to deny the possibility of cases, again both in promise and in contract, where the special obligations involved (contractual or promissory) are significant for, inter alia, their special contribution to personal relationships between the parties. The difference between contract and promise, I will argue, has to do not so much with the possibility, but with the likelihood of such cases. It has to do with the question as to whether each of the practices should be generally expected to promote personal relations in the sense which was outlined above; whether or to what extent they can be understood as *designed* to fulfil such a function, or be characterised as intrinsically valuable for their *propensity* to fulfil it.

I will argue that contract, as a practice, does not possess the same intrinsic value as promise. To recall the distinction between two principal ways in which special obligations give rise to actions that have an expressive potential, the first (and, as we shall soon see, less significant) consideration to be introduced pertains in particular to the undertaking of obligations in each of the practices.

[30] See above n 29.

[31] A contract or a promise may, most obviously, be valuable (for its parties, for the promisee) for its subject matter and not much else. But this need not be the only type of such case. A promise given to a reporter by a spokesperson, to illustrate another type, may have special value for the former as something that confirms her status as a reporter. This value need not reflect that of the subject matter of the promise (the thing promised may be of negligible significance), nor indicate or depend upon the notion that the reporter sees herself as having personal relations with the spokesperson (in any sense that transcends the fact of the promise itself).

The voluntary act of undertaking an obligation to another person (or, if you like, assuming a special obligation) can itself be instrumental in manifesting a certain range of attitudes of the kind that tends to be highly valuable in personal relationships. The particular case I have in mind is that of undertakings that are, or appear to be, altruistic. And a rather obvious, yet not too often commented-upon,[32] difference between promises and contracts may be of significance in this context: whereas contracts typically involve bilateral undertakings of obligation, a promise is a unilateral undertaking.

The unique expressive potential of altruistic undertakings of obligation to others is rather self-explanatory. The expressive content of such an act (which would, of course, be further informed by, and ultimately depend for its significance on, the particular obligation undertaken) can combine the kind of attitudes or personal attributes associated with altruistic behaviour in general, with the special commitment embodied in the self-imposition of an obligation. Now a unilateral undertaking need not be, or even appear to be, altruistic; and an altruistic undertaking need not be intended nor appear to serve the interests of its direct recipient or beneficiary (in this case, the promisee). In the discussion of promises in Chapter 1, however, although I stopped short of recognising as a conceptual truth the notion that the promisee is interested in the promise itself or in the thing promised, it was conceded that in the normal case she would be interested in both. This may reinforce the impression that, in contrast to the typically bargain-oriented contractual undertaking, a promissory undertaking could be seen as an altruistic gesture towards the promisee and, as such, attributed an expressive content that contractual undertakings would be highly unlikely to carry.

The significance of this consideration, however, must not be exaggerated. It should be suspected that once promises are placed in the kind of real-life contexts in which they are typically made, their altruistic appearance may diminish. For as we have seen, promises are typically made in the context of some on-going relationship; and often in such a context, elements of mutual dependence, prospects of individual or mutual benefit, an overlap of interests, or other structures of reciprocity can be found, rendering promises much less one-sided, much less altruistic, than they may appear to be when examined in artificial isolation. Conceding as much still leaves us well short of Patrick Atiyah's analysis of promises as admissions of already-existing obligations[33]; but it is enough to significantly undermine the consideration at stake, namely that promises are essentially altruistic. And at any rate, those writers who compare contracts to promises or who think contracts *are* promises, usually have in mind not the core case of an isolated, unilateral promise; rather, they make the sometimes seamless, yet both necessary and significant, transition to models such as 'exchange

---

[32] A notable exception is A de Moor, 'Are Contracts Promises' in J Eakelaar and J Bell (eds), *Oxford Essays in Jurisprudence* (3rd Series, Oxford, 1987).

[33] See *Promises, Morals, and Law* (Oxford, 1981) ch 7. For criticism see Raz, above n 21, at 921–27.

of promises,' 'conditional promises,' or 'exchange of conditional promises.'[34] And moving from a focus on isolated, unilateral promissory undertakings to cases where promises are exchanged or are made conditional, we often get bargain type (or close to bargain type) situations on both sides of the contract-promise divide. The remaining differences in this respect, if any, may be mainly ones of degree, emphasis, or even image. It may indeed be the case that whereas in contract the bargain is more to the fore, playing a predominant role in the image of the practice, the image of the practice of promise is largely informed by an altruistic feature the occurrence of which is but contingent.

If there are more significant differences between contract and promise in terms of their potential contribution to personal relations, such differences must lie elsewhere. They consist in elements that are, unlike altruism in promises, amongst the essential properties of the two practices. The next argument focuses on such differences. The considerations it involves can be divided in two: considerations concerning the pre-condition of transparency, and, to continue with the same metaphor, considerations concerning what is likely to be seen when transparency obtains.

The pre-condition of transparency, let us recall, usually needs to be satisfied in order for actions to carry special significance or value as manifestations of attitudes (or character traits, etc) that are themselves significant and valuable in that framework of relationship in which the actions are performed. And, in terms of transparency, the difference between the contractual framework and the non-legal, promissory domain, is stark.

Contractual relations are an extreme case of a framework in which transparency—of attitudes, of motives—would not normally obtain, or, at any rate, would normally be severely tainted. The main explanation for this has to do with enforceability, and the fairly predominant role it plays in the practice. Through creating independent reasons for discharging contractual obligations, and especially given the nature of these reasons, enforceability casts a thick and all-encompassing veil over the motives and the attitudes towards each other attributable to parties to contracts, thus leaving reliance, performance, and other aspects of contractual conduct largely devoid of expressive content.

The veil is all-encompassing since contracts typically purport to cover the entire range of actions that parties are expected to perform as parties to a contract.[35] Contracts purport to stipulate as unambiguously as possible what the

---

[34] A case in point is Fried's analysis of promise, introduced as a precursor to his analysis of contract *as* promise. Explaining the importance of the self-commitment that the practice of promise facilitates, he writes: 'More central to our concern is the situation where we facilitate each other's projects, where the gain is reciprocal. Schematically, the situation looks like this: You want to accomplish purpose A and I want to accomplish purpose B. Neither of us can succeed without the cooperation of the other. Thus I want to be able to commit myself to help you achieve A so that you will commit yourself to help me achieve B.' (*Contract as Promise* (Cambridge, Massachusetts, 1981) 13)

[35] For a comment on possible exceptions see below, on personal detachment and relational contracts.

obligations of each party are, setting precise timetables, procedures, and means for discharging them. A good, carefully-drafted contract is one that admits as few gaps as possible. Inasmuch as it involves futurity, such a contract would also purport to anticipate all the circumstances and combinations of circumstances which could give rise to a default in the course of its implementation, and stipulate, again leaving as little room as possible for interpretation or gap-filling, what should be done in every such case. Of course law reports are strewn with cases where this has not been achieved; but inasmuch as it is thought that circumstances which prove to require interpretation of (or gap-filling in) a contract could reasonably have been foreseen, the failure to provide for these in advance is normally considered to be, indeed, a failure. To recall our (impossible) story about the 'friend' who got hold of *The Comprehensive Guide to Friendship*, it could be said that contracts are typically intended, as far as the relations between their parties are concerned, to serve as a similar guide. But if it were thought that the person who (to his friends' knowledge) regularly consults *The Comprehensive Guide* would find that her ability to express appropriate attitudes or dispositions through discharging her special responsibilities is very limited, then parties to contract are far more limited in this respect. After all the contract, unlike the guide in the original story, does more than merely identify all the relevant obligations and stipulate how and when they should be discharged. Implicit (at least) and often explicit[36] in it are also the precise consequences that each party would face if it (unjustifiably) fails to perform its obligations. And although remedies for breach usually aim to compensate the innocent party for its loss and not to punish the defaulting party or strip it of its profits (that is, the profits accrued through the breach),[37] the latter is typically (part of) their practical effect. The availability of remedies seriously and manifestly reduces the likelihood that, and at any rate the extent to which, a party would benefit from a breach, significantly undermining the expressive potential of contractual fidelity in the process.[38]

[36] To the extent that the contract contains remedial stipulations, eg marking out certain terms as conditions the breach of which gives rise to the right to rescind, including or excluding certain remedies, setting liquidated damages, etc.

[37] This is the common law's position. See generally GH Treitel, *The Law of Contract* (10th edn, London, 1999) 864–79 (for a brief account of exceptions to this rule (ie cases where the damages awarded are intended to strip the party in breach of its gains) see also at 866–69). For a critical discussion of 'disgorgement of profits' damages see LD Smith, 'Disgorgement of the Profits of Breach of Contract' (1994–5) 24 *Can Bus LJ* 121; and see discussion of remedies in Chapter 4.

[38] Note that this line of argument does not depend for its validity on the theoretical rejection of, nor on the actual reluctance by the legal system to uphold, the 'efficient breach' approach. A system of contract law that seeks to enable or encourage an efficient breach would at least make (certain types of) a breach legitimate *subject to compensation*, aimed to ensure that the innocent party is not worse off as a result of the breach—part and parcel of the very concept of efficiency in this context. In such a framework, enforceability would still serve as a deterrent to conduct that fails to meet fixed contractual standards (eg a breach combined with a failure to compensate), and have similar effects (to those discussed in the text) in terms of transparency and expressive potential with regard to actions required by *its* conception of contractual fidelity. It is interesting to note that Alan Schwartz has argued, from an economic perspective, that the standard remedy that would be most conducive

Bearing in mind that remedies for breach are administered by the purposely designed and conspicuously powerful mechanisms of the legal system, we can also see in what sense the veil that is cast over the motives and the attitudes which underpin contractual conduct can be said to be a thick one. The point to be made here is equivalent to one made in an earlier discussion, when the detrimental effect of legal threats on the expressive potential of obedience was examined in relation to criminal law and the relationship between authority and its subjects.[39] It is that enforceability does not only create independent reasons for performance, but that these reasons are clearly meant to be, and usually are, strong enough to motivate action all by themselves, and strong enough to outweigh (most types of) conflicting reasons or motives.

In the present context it might be worth reiterating that the point is not that in the presence of the kind of powerful 'external' reasons that the legal framework provides, conforming actions—and here, mainly, discharging contractual obligations—could only be understood as motivated by such reasons. The similarly exaggerated view that, in the presence of a threat, '[f]or all we know . . . compliance was motivated by fear of sanction' has been rejected.[40] Rather, the situation is typically one where we simply do not know. But such ambiguity, bearing in mind that it is the product of the very nature of the practice and the institutions it involves and that it reflects the practice's mode of operation in the very circumstances in which it is normally expected to function (ie transactions made outside the framework of already-existing personal relationships), is enough to mark the contractual framework out as a singularly inadequate arena for revealing character traits and expressing attitudes of the kind on which personal relationships thrive.

There is no equivalent problem of transparency in promise. As usual in life—and, in particular, in cases where people partake in practices that are in large part moulded by intricate social institutions and conventions, and that are further complicated and informed by the personal relationships in the context of which such practices are invoked—transparency here may rarely be complete. We have seen, for instance, that in certain circumstances a promise-breaker would be likely to face adverse consequences, something that could, if known to others, taint the transparency of the attitudes or motives behind her keeping the promise and undermine the expressive content or the symbolic significance that such an act would otherwise convey; and that in other circumstances, keeping a promise may be tightly knit into the prospect of receiving some future benefit, with a similar effect in terms of transparency and expressive potential. Yet we have also seen that the various elements which could taint transparency in the

---

to facilitating efficient breach scenarios is in fact specific performance. (See 'The Case for Specific Performance' (1979) 89 *Yale Law Journal* 271). For a powerful critique of the 'efficient breach' approach see D Friedmann, 'The Efficient Breach Fallacy' (1989) 18 *Journal of Legal Studies* 1; and see discussion of remedies in Chapter 4.

[39] See Chapter 2 on threats and expressive reasons.

[40] See *ibid.*

non-legal, promissory framework, are by and large contingent, and often highly speculative. And even when present, the independent reasons (for keeping promises, for relying on promises) such elements amount to or entail would only rarely (and, again, contingently) match, in terms of actual and apparent motivating force, the kind of equivalent independent reasons that the law purports to produce.

Transparency, however, is but a pre-condition. What marks promise out as a practice that possesses the intrinsic value that lies in its ability to enhance personal relations is the kind of messages that it is particularly suitable for conveying when transparency obtains. From earlier discussions of the normative foundations of this practice, we already know what these are. We saw in what sense promises depend for their normal functioning on the existence of, on the one hand, (non-trivial) personal trust, and, on the other, respect. We saw in what sense it is the case that, in normal conditions, to make a promise is to invite personal trust, and to accept the promise, take it seriously and rely on it is to give that trust; and we saw (through the comparison between promise-breaking and lying) why to break (unjustifiably) a promise is to demonstrate lack of respect—in that Kantian, morally significant sense—for the promisee. Through the completed circle of a promise made, relied upon, and kept, messages can be conveyed and reassurances can be gained that these ingredients, trust and respect, are present in a relationship.[41]

We can now add that the personal attributes and the attitudes towards others that promises help express have a unique status amongst the various potential building blocks of personal relations. Unlike many other attitudes and character traits which would normally be *welcome* in *most* types of personal relations, and which are *sometimes* straightforwardly *necessary* in the contexts of certain types of relations, trust, trustworthiness, and respect are fundamental, necessary conditions probably for all forms of meaningful personal relationship. People who are generally incapable of earning other people's trust, people who can never trust others, and people who do not have basic respect for (at least certain) others, would seem generally incapable of having meaningful personal relations. Thus the practice of promising provides a framework within which people can habitually demonstrate, emphasise, and reassert their basic capacity, or at least some central elements of the capacity, to have personal relations.

To conclude, whereas contractual relations are a singularly inadequate framework in which to express attitudes and reveal personal attributes of the kind that tend to create and enhance personal relationships, promises are uniquely suited to this very purpose.[42] Before proceeding, I wish to emphasise

---

[41] A similar idea (I think) was phrased nicely by Dan-Cohen: '[T]he reciprocal relation between trust and deference can be seen as a transaction that creates surplus value measured in the denomination of individual's self-respect.' ('In Defence of Defiance' (1994) 23 *Philosophy and Public Affairs* 24, at 40). The point was made in the context of an argument focusing on 'the importance of being trusted,' illustrated with the case of the 'honour system' of examination (hence the emphasis on *self* respect).

[42] On promises and the *creation* of personal relations, see also Chapter 1 on promises between strangers.

again that, as mentioned at the outset, my argument was not meant to imply that all promises promote personal relationships, or that contractual relations never give rise to or develop into relationships that extend over and beyond—in meaning, significance and value—the agreed terms of the contract itself. The argument is about what functions each of the practices can reasonably be understood as designed to fulfil, about the values it should, and those it should not, be generally expected to promote. At the risk of exaggerating the point somewhat, it could be said that contracts sometimes generate or reinforce personal relationships despite the way in which the practice operates, whereas promises, despite the way in which this practice operates, sometimes *fail* to do the same thing.

The Intrinsic Value of Contracts

The discussion thus far may have created the impression that contract, as a practice, is simply less valuable than promise. For I have argued that whereas the two practices share a similar instrumental function, only promise possesses the additional value that lies in its potential contribution to personal relationships. Moreover, the inadequacy of contract as a means of enhancing personal relationships was explained, in a sense, as a price paid for the practice's mode of operation in fulfilling its instrumental function: the legal system, through the special sources of reassurance it provides, alleviates the burden of personal trust which promises normally require in order to fulfil their instrumental function, thus broadening the range of circumstances in which contracts can fulfil a similar function; but at the same time, it is the very introduction of such special sources of reassurance that accounts for the loss of the capacity to enhance personal relationships the way promises tend to do. And yet, as I will now explain, to conclude that contracts are plainly *less* valuable—to conclude that, in contrast to promise, contract has no intrinsic value—would be a gross error. In fact, the distinct, intrinsic value of contract has been emerging gradually throughout the discussion thus far. All that needs doing now is to point out that it is indeed a thing of value.

The comparison with promise not only reveals that the legal practice of contract does not possess the same intrinsic value as its non-legal equivalent; it also provides the key to the intrinsic value that the practice does possess. This value is very different indeed from that of promise: it is, in a sense, the diametrically opposed value. It consists in the very framework contracts provide for doing certain things with others not only outside the context of already-existing relationships, but also without a commitment to the future prospect of such relationships, without being required to know much or form opinions about the personal attributes of others, and without having to allow others to know much and form opinions about oneself. It is, if you like, the value of personal detachment.

It may come as a surprise that two features as diametrically opposed as personal relationships and personal detachment can both be considered good things, and practices that are capable of promoting only one of them—and not the same one—can both be considered valuable for this very reason. But it should not. Not only is it easy to see that, when examined in isolation, both personal relationships and personal detachment can be, in the right circumstances, a good thing, but in fact when the two co-exist as options in people's lives, their respective values tend to be mutually reinforcing.

Personal relations are more valuable, or are likely to be more valuable, the greater the freedom people enjoy and the more selective they can be in pursuing them; whereas the more dependent people are on personal relations for the pursuit of goals that are themselves external to such relations, and the less selective they are allowed to be in creating, developing, and maintaining their personal relations, the less valuable the relations they have are likely to be. Of course, certain kinds of personal relations do not depend for their value on the parties' unlimited freedom to pursue or to mould them. Some relations exclude certain significant choices by nature—relations between family members, to take an extreme example, exclude choices concerning the identity of the other party—while still being, potentially, highly valuable. But as a general observation about personal relations, the point remains valid. Note that even where examples such as family relations are concerned, the relative freedom to draw lines, to exert control over the scope, the depth and the intensity of the relationship usually tends to improve the quality of the relationship and enhance its value for the parties, rendering it more meaningful—indeed, it is tempting to say more viable—than the kind of all-encompassing family ties that deny the parties the opportunity to maintain relative privacy or detachment in any way or with regard to any aspect of their lives.

Similar reasoning applies where the value of personal detachment is concerned. It is precisely when people are capable of having valuable personal relations that their ability to do things with others without having to get personally involved is valued. Detachment is valuable as an option, not a predicament; and as such it is valuable as an alternataive to dependence on (pre-existing, future) personal relations. And contracts are valuable as a practice that, with regard to a certain range of activities, facilitates this very option.

If you like, contract emerges not *as promise*, but as a *substitute for* promise. The difference may seem subtle, yet I believe it to be crucial. For it represents the abandonment of the over-simplified notion that the law can systematically replicate existing moral or social institutions or simply enforce the rights or the obligations to which they give rise, without altering these institutions in the process and while leaving their functions and values intact. This over-simplification, we can now see, can result not only in a failure to appreciate possible drawbacks or inadequacies of the legal framework, but also in a failure to acknowledge the law's unique, actual or potential strengths. In contract, the law offers a genuine alternative to promise: a practice that, in instrumental terms, can be expected to fulfil a similar role, but that is particularly suited for fulfill-ing this role in different circumstances and while bringing into play different, indeed diametrically opposed, intrinsic qualities.

In Chapter 1, we encountered Charles Fried's account of the value of promise as deriving from the promotion of freedom.[43] My conclusions regarding con-tract, and the difference between this practice and promise, could be expressed in a similar currency. By providing a framework for the voluntary assumption of obligations, thus facilitating the co-ordinated or joint pursuit of potentially valuable projects and goals, contract promotes a certain type of freedom—one the promotion of which, as Fried showed, is equally attributable to promise. But as a facilitator of personal detachment, the legal practice of contract is a source of yet another, very different freedom: the freedom from dependence upon the very institution—personal relationship—in the enhancement of which lies the intrinsic value of the practice's non-legal equivalent.

Personal Detachment and Relational Contracts

I can anticipate a growing sense of anxiety amongst certain readers—those who are familiar with the concept of, and the debate in the literature about, rela-tional contracts. The concept and its theory owe their high profile mainly to Ian Macneil's fascinating and highly original writing on the theory of contract, and have been at the centre of a lively theoretical debate at least since the publica-tion, in the mid-1970s, of his influential article 'The Many Futures of Contract.'[44] While I could not possibly do justice to the intricacy of this subject in the confines of the present work, in this section I wish to comment briefly on the sources of the anticipated anxiety, and to indicate why I believe that it should not be felt after all. If nothing else, this should provide me with another opportunity to illustrate the role and the significance of personal detachment in contract, and to illustrate the notion that personal detachment and personal relations can be mutually reinforcing.

My greatest difficulty here will be to introduce the concept of relational con-tract to those who are not familiar with the related, highly diverse literature. The main reason for this is that the literature, generated primarily (though not solely) by law and economics scholarship,[45] does not speak in one voice. Not

---

[43] See ch 1, n 49 and text.

[44] (1974) 47 *Southern California Law Review* 691. See also his 'Economic Analysis of Contractual Relations' (1981) 75 *Northwestern University Law Review* 1018. For other notable contributions, see eg CJ Goetz and RE Scott, 'Principles of Relational Contracts' (1981) 67 *Virginia Law Review* 1089; A Schwartz, 'Relational Contracts in the Courts: An Analysis of Incomplete Agreements and Judicial Strategies' (1992) 21 *Journal of Legal Studies* 21. For a useful overview see 'Introduction' in *Macneil, Selected Works*, chs 1–3 (by D Campbell, J Feinman and P Vincent-Jones).

[45] See *ibid*, but also MA Eisenberg, 'Relational Contracts' and E McKendrick, 'The Regulation of Long-Term Contracts in English Law,' both in J Beatson and D Friedmann (eds), *Good Faith and Fault in Contract Law* (Oxford, 1995) 291, 305; and see Hugh Collins' comment on the subject in *Regulating Contract* (Oxford, 1999) 140–43.

only are the precise rules that apply or should apply to relational contracts, and the implications of the phenomenon to any particular area of contract theory and contract law, the subjects of on-going debate and much controversy, but so are the very definition, and the very possibility of a definition, of the term 'relational contract.'[46] Indeed, the possibility of a precise definition should be doubted for at least two reasons. First, the 'relational contract' has been commonly introduced as a rival, and its theory as a reaction, to the 'discrete contract,' a term or a paradigm the precise definition of which is itself rather illusive.[47] Secondly, it would be risky to try and clump together, under a single definition, all contracts or contractual relations that could be described as 'relational,' if only because different contracts or contractual relations can be relational in various senses and to highly varying degrees.

Still, it should be possible to identify the gist of the concept, and to investigate its compatibility with the argument of the previous section. It is tempting to start with Eisenberg's proposed definition of a relational contract as, simply, one 'that involves not merely an exchange, but also a relationship, between the parties.'[48] The crux of the matter is that the relationship in question can, and is often expected by the parties to, generate a wealth of norms, define or inform expectations, provide sources of reassurance, facilitate co-operation, create interdependence, and so on—over and above, and, indeed, potentially instead of, what can be gleaned from the contract or contracts to which they are parties, and over and above what is provided by the bare legal norms and legal mechanisms that underlie or support these contracts in the relevant jurisdiction.[49]

The clear examples of relational contracts typically (though, as Goetz and Scott explained, not by definition) involve a long-term contractual involvement between the parties.[50] The paradigmatic examples are contractual relations

---

[46] See eg discussion by Eisenberg, *ibid*, and references there.

[47] *Ibid* at 296–97.

[48] *Ibid* at 296.

[49] For a brief comment on this particular aspect of relational contracts see my discussion of the freedom from contract in Chapter 5.

[50] 'Principles of Relational Contracts,' above n 44, at 1089–91. Though I am by no means suggesting that these are the only examples of relational contracts, I wish to distance myself from the view of those who tend to vastly exaggerate the scope of the phenomenon. While Macneil's early observations about the 'relational' aspects of certain classes of contract were greeted with often unwarranted scepticism, and Macneil himself has always been rather cautious in acknowledging the scope of non-relational contracts (see eg *Macneil, Selected Works*, at 23), some contemporary writers argue, often on the basis of the flimsiest of evidence, that most, or nearly all contracts are relational. Eisenberg, for instance, wrote that 'it is discrete contracts that are unusual, not relational contracts,' so that 'contracts that involve a relationship between the contracting parties, beyond a mere relationship of strangerhood, comprise the bread and butter of contracting' (above n 45, 297–98). A lot depends, of course, on what precisely 'relational contracts' are taken to be: under a watered-down definition that reduces the concept to the point of meaninglessness (or, similarly, under an impossibly strict definition of 'discrete contract'), all contracts might indeed be said to display some relational aspects. As none of my arguments (thus far, and those to follow) depends for its validity on the refutation of any such view, this is not the time to address the issue in any detail. Looking around the room I could point out, however, that the computer on which these words are written, the apartment in which I live, the car I drove here this morning and the mobile phone that has just stopped ringing were all purchased through one-off, non-personal contractual transactions

involving or pertaining to franchises, joint ventures, employment, distributorship, and the like.[51] In such types of relationship, it is easy to appreciate how the parties may be involved with each other in ways that far transcend formal contract or its immediate legal implications. They may be dependent on each other for the pursuit of long-term projects and goals over and above the subject matter of any particular contract or contracts to which they are parties; they may be familiar with each other's strengths, weaknesses, and vulnerabilities, possibly in ways that allow them continually to adjust their mutual expectations, enhance their co-operation or better co-ordinate their actions; they may operate in an environment where reputation often counts for far more than the gains to be had from an opportunistic breach of contract or from a successful legal action, and where the repercussions of underhand practices in terms of reputation lost may be far greater than those which could be brought about through any legal action taken against them.

This rough characterisation should suffice to reveal what I see as a potential source of anxiety. For I argued that the intrinsic value of contract lies in the very detachment between parties that it facilitates—detachment that can find its expression in, among other things, avoiding precisely the kind of involvement described in the previous paragraph as characteristic of relational contracts. Moreover, the enforceability of contracts was described as a significant contributor to the value of personal detachment, whereas, as with many other features of formal contract, the role of enforceability in the context of relational contracts is often highly diminished. Both as a source of reassurance and as a source of external pressure or motivation, it often plays but a secondary role to, and sometimes fades to complete insignificance beside, the kind of equivalent sources of reassurance and motivation that can be found in the relational context.

I said earlier that it would be wrong to treat all relational contracts as one category, and that contracts can be relational in various senses and, importantly, to varying degrees. At one extreme end of the spectrum of relationality, so to speak, we may find parties whose mutual involvement (or interdependence, or mutual resolve to co-operate successfully even in the face of serious difficulty, etc) is such that the contract (or contracts) to which they are parties serve, in practice, as not

---

that cannot be said to be (or to have become) 'relational' in any significant sense. That holds true even for the long-term aspects of some such contracts, such as the warranty and servicing agreement that came with the computer or the car, or the line-rental and billing agreement that comes with a mobile phone. The fact that the manufacturer's obligations in this respect are enshrined in formal, enforceable contract, (as opposed to the goodwill of the service department's personnel, or anyone's concern for their or their company's reputation, etc), far from being insignificant, remains the main source of confidence that they will be discharged, as anyone who has tried to deal personally with the service department of, say, Dell Computers, or the billing department of a mobile phone's service provider will know only too well. Multiply the number of such contracts that an average person enters by the number of average persons in any given jurisdiction, and the claim that *most* contracts are relational appears to be highly tenuous indeed.

[51] See Goetz and Scott, above n 44.

much more than an informal memorandum, or, in case of difficulty or misunderstanding, serve as but a loose starting point for re-negotiation and adjustment. All that can be said about such relations is that they are, indeed, relational, but hardly *contractual*—or, if you want, they are relational *to the point of* not being contractual—or, at any rate, not contractual in any significant sense. There is of course nothing wrong in parties deciding to mould and pursue their relations in a way that renders formal contract entirely (or almost entirely) insignificant, and to eschew altogether the option of legal enforceability, alongside any number of other facilities or mechanisms with which the legal system furnishes them as parties to contract. But the very possibility (or reality) of such relations poses no challenge to a theory of contract, mine or any other that I could think of; much in the same way that the fact that some people choose to buy cars and never drive them poses no challenge to a theory that depicts the value of cars as lying, inter alia, in their usefulness as means of transport. This remains true, at least, so long as the attitude in question (eg not driving cars) does not become the predominant approach to the practice or institution that the theory seeks to explain. And since this is clearly not the case with the extreme examples of relational contract and the institution of contracting, suffice it to emphasise that my argument was that the intrinsic value of contract lies in the opportunity with which it provides parties to deal at arm's length and maintain detachment *if they so wish*. It need not prevent parties from doing otherwise, and doing otherwise may indeed be desirable and valuable or even inevitable in certain circumstances.

But let us dwell no further on the extreme cases, for cases falling short of the extreme end of the spectrum are not only more plentiful, but their analysis is also more instructive for the purposes of a theory *of contract*. Now the proviso I have just emphasised—*if they so wish*—remains important in assessing the role and value of personal detachment when attention is shifted away from the most extreme cases of relationality. However in this new context, much more can be said. For in many, indeed in the paradigmatic examples of relational contract, the personal detachment that the contractual framework affords, far from merely an irrelevance or simply an option that parties choose to eschew, can be and often is highly conducive to the very development and prosperity of relational dimensions. The thought that I have expressed before, namely that personal detachment and personal relations tend to be mutually reinforcing—and sometimes so in the framework of one relationship—often finds its clearest illustration in precisely this type of case: it is the very fact that the contract provides for some more or less certain, enforceable fundamentals, that liberates the parties from dependence on the creation or maintenance of personal relations for the realisation of such fundamentals; and this liberty, in turn, is often indispensable in enabling the parties to develop, possibly over time, a relationship that far transcends that set of legally binding rights and duties which the contract constituted or recorded in the first place.

I wish to make these thoughts more tangible with the help of one example. Various types of employment relations provide rich illustrations of relational contracts. Of course not all types of employment, or even long-term employ-ment, are the same in this respect: employer-employee relationships can vary widely in every respect, including as to whether or the extent to which they embody or give rise to relational dimensions over and above the contractual ones. But a particularly good example (and good not only in light of my personal familiarity with it) is that of employment relations in academia. These typically provide particularly powerful illustrations of relational contracts for a variety of reasons, and let me name but a few. Academic careers tend to be motivated ideologically to a considerable extent. Far from 'just a job,' academics tend to see their work (in terms of commitment to teaching, to research, and so on) as a central, on-going life project. They tend to identify with their academic institu-tions, and with these institutions' ambitions and goals, in a way and to an extent that significantly undercuts rough and ready distinctions between employer's and employee's interests and aspirations. The spirit that typically drives these relationships is predominantly one of partaking in a joint effort, much more so, at least, than that of the self-interested furthering of individual interests.

There are probably as many symptoms of this phenomenon as there are reasons for it. For example, probably more so than in any other market sector, academics (tenured ones included) are habitually asked, routinely agree, and not infrequently volunteer, to undertake additional tasks or adopt new procedures that translate into significant increases in their workload but not into a pay rise. They routinely forgo opportunities to engage in more profitable or less demand-ing employ outside academia. And, to concentrate on the ostensibly *contractual* aspects of the relationship, these normally appear to be fairly minimal indeed. The employment contract is hardly ever consulted in the course of an aca-demic's professional life, and its role in shaping her daily routine as an employee, as well as in determining the overall trajectory of her career, appears to be decidedly limited. Even inasmuch as the contract purports to set out the precise range of duties and responsibilities that an academic job involves (in terms of teaching load, research responsibilities, and the like), in reality aca-demic jobs tend to develop a life of their own, and involve much more, and much that is simply different, than is prescribed in the contract.

Yet even in such a relationship, the contract, and with it the scope for per-sonal detachment it affords, fulfils a continuing function whose significance must not be overlooked—a function which is crucial for the development, the thriving, and the stability of relational dimensions. It may play a seemingly very limited role in, so to speak, the life of the relationship, but it is predominant in its inception and, potentially, its death. And in between, it merely fades into the background, but as such helps to sustain the very background against which, and only against which, all that happens in between can happen.

In slightly greater detail, this (admittedly somewhat simplified) three-part story looks more or less like this. Following a successful interview, an academic job is offered, often in a letter or over the phone. A short negotiation will some-times follow, pertaining to a limited range of issues such as starting salary and the like. When these are agreed, a contract is sent, and the new recruit is asked to sign both copies and return one. The more scrupulous ones will read through carefully before signing, and possibly ask for clarification where the legal language of the document is too obscure, or for some minor alterations. The great majority, I suspect, look briefly through the document, sign on the dotted line, and place their copy in a drawer.

And in the drawer it is likely to stay for a long time, for the contract will have precious little motivation and precious little guidance to provide for the way in which an academic interacts with students, colleagues, administrative staff, deans and heads of departments; the way in which she approaches teaching, research, undertaking and performing administrative tasks; her pursuit and development of rich, meaningful collegiate relations, both with her immediate colleagues and with fellow scholars from farther afield; her showing interest in and providing feedback on other academic's research; her continuing endeavour to improve various aspects of her performance as a teacher and a scholar; and many more of the most significant aspects of her professional life.

What role does personal detachment have to play in this phase of the relationship? The answer is simple. The greater the extent to which all those activities, interactions, and personal relationships that an academic typically pursues in her professional life could have a direct bearing on fundamentals such as the length of her tenure, her entitlement to pension, the terms under which she may leave her current place of employ or the conditions under which she may be dismissed, the less she can genuinely engage in such pursuits and the less, in the course of such pursuits, she can develop true, meaningful relationships. Motives and attitudes could be tainted, expressive content obscured, and so on. And relative immunity from such hindrances can be found in precisely the sort of detachment, albeit often fragmented and less than entirely robust, that the contract (alongside, in this case, various other legal instruments, such as legislation or the institution's constitution, which together define the legal framework of the relationship) provides.

And it provides it for all parties. For if the 'relational' aspects of the contract were all-encompassing, and the parties did not enjoy the relative immunity from dependence upon them for the realisation of those fundamentals for which the contractual dimension of the relationship provides, then not only the employee but many others with whom she interacts in her professional life would be seriously hindered in their endeavour (inasmuch as it is their endeavour) to reach beyond formal contract and to develop true personal bonds. A dean, for instance, or head of department, would likely find herself rather inhibited in her efforts to develop an informal friendship with a new appointee, if she knows that their interactions invariably lead to understandings or expectations pertaining to those issues that formal contract settles.

The fact that, as I put it earlier, during the life of the relationship the contract (and with it the scope for personal detachment it affords) merely fades into the background, often receives a vivid reminder if or when the relationship enters the third stage, its breakdown. For when the time comes for employee and employer to part ways, it is not unusual for the contract to be taken out of the drawer or off the shelf on which it has been gathering dust, and be expected to provide the precise procedures to be followed. Not necessarily, of course: when an academic wishes to resign, for instance, the length of the notice period she must provide may be amicably and informally agreed. Yet often in this context, the contract will be thrust back to the fore. The employee would likely consult the provisions it supplies for the breakdown of the relationship, including the length of the notice period, before she hands in her resignation; and if she does not, and half way through an academic term she informs her head of department that she is leaving next week, the latter would most likely consult the contract and suggest otherwise. And even when terms are agreed amicably and co-operatively, the contract is likely to be consulted by both parties, and serve, if nothing else, as the starting point for adjustment or compromise.

The protagonist I had in mind when introducing this example was the tenured academic. The limited-term contracts under which untenured academics are employed naturally provide far less scope for personal detachment of the kind I described, for at least inasmuch as the academic in question is hoping to be tenured, the contractual aspects of the relationship would not provide for what is for her the most pressing of all concerns. And indeed, untenured academics often find themselves in a situation where, potentially at least, every aspect of their performance in an academic institution, and every feature of the relations they succeed or fail to establish with colleagues, superiors, and even students, could have an impact on the one decision that will matter most. The important role that personal detachment plays in relational contracts could explain why, over and above the obvious matter of possible differences in terms of the actual duration of the relationship, it would normally be harder, if anything, for genuine relational dimensions to develop in the context of such employment relations than it is in the context of tenured academic employment, with the far greater scope for personal detachment that the latter allows.

Preview

Although the discussion thus far has been pursued at a rather theoretical level, its conclusions may have a bearing on a range of issues of a more practical nature. After all, an understanding of the nature of contract, its true functions and true value, forms an important part of the background against which to understand and interpret the obligations contractual relations involve, and against which to investigate the roles designated for, and the principles of action applying to, the institutions the contractual framework comprises. Especially when pitched against predominant theoretical trends that have traditionally failed to pay heed to the crucial differences between the legal practice and its non-legal equivalent, the implications that flow from an analysis of the dissimilarities of value and function between the two may prove to be of some significance. In the next two chapters, some such implications will hopefully come to light.

Implications pertaining to issues arising within contract law will surface in the next chapter, where I will discuss the choice of standard remedy for breach of contract. Implications pertaining to broader questions of policy should emerge in Chapter 5, where I will examine the political ideal of freedom of contract, and suggest supplementing it with another ideal of a strong liberal orientation, that of freedom *from* contract. These discussions will not only serve to illustrate the practical significance of the argument thus far, but should also provide an opportunity for its further elucidation.

And yet, in the discussions of all but one of these issues, my argument concerning the difference in terms of intrinsic function and value between contract and promise will not take centre stage. By contrast, the liberal underpinnings of my approach will be brought to the fore. Thus the focal point of the discussion of remedies will be the implications for this issue of one of the principal tenets of modern liberalism, namely John Stuart Mill's 'harm principle'; and in discussing the freedom of contract, I will argue that the erroneous association of liberalism with a particularly rigid conception of this freedom and with a doctrine that allows a very limited role to the state in shaping and regulating contractual activity, is owed in large part to a misconception of liberalism itself, and only in small part to a misconception of contract and its relationship with promise. But the relatively modest (though by no means insignificant) role that the argument concerning the difference between contract and promise will play in these discussions should not come as a surprise, nor as a disappointment. For nowhere in the discussion thus far has it been suggested that contract and promise are not similar in any way (in fact, the similarities between the two, and not just the differences, have been specifically accounted for), or that the differences between them explain everything that needs to be explained with regard to contract or contract law (rather, much can be explained by reference to the similarities). And, at any rate, placing the direct implications of the argument concerning the unique characteristics of contract in the broader context of liberal theory should be conducive, not detrimental, to an attempt to elucidate it, as well as to lend it further support.

4

Remedies

———◦◦———

I HAVE ARGUED THAT contract has two main functions, and that accordingly the practice should be understood as possessing two distinct values: an instrumental function and value that it shares with promise, and an intrinsic function and value that are diametrically opposed to those of promise, and that lie in its ability to facilitate personal detachment. In the course of arguing along these lines, I alluded on more than one occasion to the popular view that the core contractual obligation (and hence, for that matter, the core contractual right) is analogous to that at the heart of promise, namely performance; or, to recall Daniel Friedmann's phrase, the view that the *essence* of contract is performance.[1]

Whereas none of my arguments concerning the true functions and value of contract depended for their validity on the truth of that view, I believe that they provide it with credence. This belief will be borne out in this chapter, where I will approach the issue of remedies for breach of contract mostly by way of addressing a long-standing debate concerning the apparent discord between the view that the core contractual right and obligation are performance, and the remedial rights that are in practice recognised (and the corresponding duties that are imposed) in this area of the law. Several preliminary concerns, however, will have to be addressed first. Chief amongst them is the very notion that considerations such as those that emerged in previous chapters *could* have a bearing on the issue of remedies for breach. As we shall see, this notion itself has been the subject of some controversy.

The Standard Remedy and the Theory of the Practice

Having used the term *core* contractual obligation (or, similarly, core contractual right), I mentioned an apparent discord, in contract law, between it and remedial rights. (From hereon I will sometimes omit the separate reference to duties, though my subsequent comments should be equally applicable to both.) But remedies for breach of contract come in numerous shapes and forms. Is there scope for speaking of the core remedial right (or, similarly, the core

[1] 'The Performance Interest in Contract Damages' (1995) 111 *Law Quarterly Review* 628, at 629.

remedial duty)? Is there a point in asking what is, or what should be, the *stand-ard* remedial response to a breach?

I think there is. It is true that the great diversity of types of contract and con-tractual relations, and the greater diversity still of circumstances in which con-tractual disputes arise, mean that whatever the answers might be, there are bound to be numerous cases where the standard remedy would prove to be under- or over-compensatory, impractical, or otherwise unfair or inappropri-ate. Nevertheless, such questions can, and should, be asked. Answering them may be understood as an attempt to determine what is (or what should be) the general rule and what should count as a justification-requiring deviation from it, allowing that instances where deviations from the rule could be justified may be many. But there is no reason to assume in advance that no grounds for a gen-eral rule could be found. Moreover, a grasp of the rule and *its* justification may well prove conducive to understanding what kind of considerations could just-ify deviating from it. Contrary to the popular saying, exceptions cannot prove the rule; at best they can prove that the rule has exceptions. But the nature of and the reasons for the rule may well have a role to play in explaining both the need and the legitimate grounds for exceptions.

How are we to go about the task of discovering the grounds for the general rule? Where should we look first when we try to find out what the standard rem-edy for breach of contract should be? Intuitively, I would say that the starting point should be the underlying theory of the practice. Our understanding of the nature of the practice—the main functions that it should or should not be expected to fulfil, the nature and the normative foundations of the rights and the duties it encompasses—is surely highly pertinent to a critical examination of the measures to be taken when the rights to which it gives rise are violated or the duties recognised by it are not discharged. Such an intuition can be explained a bit further. Remedies are likely to have two main, related, functions: to protect the practice itself against erosion and debasement, and to protect those engag-ing in the practice against harm.[2] And these two functions are clearly linked to the underlying theory of the practice. Our understanding of the practice's main functions and values is surely amongst the things that explain what would, and what would not, amount to its erosion or debasement. It may also indicate what courses of action are to be taken in order to prevent such occurrences. Similarly, it is mainly (if not only) on the basis of an understanding of the practice's func-tions and values, and hence the (legitimate) purposes for which parties may put it into use, that we may determine what should (and what should not) count as harm to contracting parties, or, at any rate, as harm that merits legal protec-

---

[2] For a similar point see J Raz, 'Book Review: Promises in Morality and Law' (1982) 95 *Harvard Law Review* 916, at 933–38. The two functions are related because the protection of the practice is achieved, at least in part (and plausibly for the most part), through the protection of contracting par-ties, and, to some extent, vice versa: the protection of the practice against at least certain forms of erosion and debasement would tend to decrease the likelihood that individuals acting in it will be harmed as a result. This point is resumed later in the text.

tion—considerations which, in turn, may well be relevant for deciding on the shape that such protection, when due, should take.

Yet intuitive or straightforward as it may seem to be, the link between the nature of the practice or the theory that purports to explain it and the choice of remedies for breach, while taken for granted by some, has been overlooked, and in some cases directly challenged, by others. Perhaps most curious is the view that acknowledges the link, but suggests that it works the other way round, namely from remedies to the nature of the practice, or, more specifically, to the nature of the rights and the duties that lie at its heart. Such an approach can be traced back to the work of Oliver Wendell Holmes,[3] but it has echoes in contemporary literature as well. Atiyah, for instance, lists as one of Holmes' 'insights' the notion (which, Atiyah claims, is also the starting point for Lon Fuller's influential contribution to modern contract theory) that 'it is impossible sensibly to discuss *how* binding a contract is until one knows what form of damages are likely to be awarded for its breach,'[4] and, referring to Fuller, states approvingly that 'it was . . . he himself who first demonstrated the extent to which the rights of a contracting party are in practice *determined by* the differing kinds of damages that he may recover.'[5]

Unless the emphasis in this last quote is understood to be on the 'in practice,' Atiyah would seem to confuse what is a common strategy of legal reasoning with the real issue of logical priority. The common or the legal response to a violation of right can at best be indicative of the nature of that right, or of the way that right is commonly or legally perceived. It cannot, however, 'determine' what the right is—or what it should be—in any deeper, normative, sense.

More pervasive than the 'remedies before rights' approach are arguments that deny or seek to expose the limitedness of the impact that the underlying theory of contractual obligation has, or should have, on the question of remedies. 'Arguments' is perhaps the wrong word to use in this context, because very few have actually tried to offer an argument to this effect. In their celebrated 'The Reliance Interest in Contract Damages,' Fuller and Perdue, for instance, seem simply to assume that the reasons to hold that contracts create obligations (something which is, itself, a proposition they accepted) are of little consequence for the discussion of remedies.[6] A rare attempt to *argue* that questions of remedies (as well as many other issues arising in contract law) sometimes can and should be addressed independently of 'philosophical theories' of contract law was made by Richard Craswell,[7] focusing in particular on the presumed bearing

---

[3] Aptly described by Daniel Friedmann as 'an attempt to view the contractual right through the looking glass of the damages awarded for its breach.' See D Friedmann, 'The Performance Interest in Contract Damages,' above n 1; and see references there, at n 7.

[4] PS Atiyah, *Essays on Contract* (Oxford, 1986) Essay 3: 'Holmes and the Theory of Contract,' 57, at 61 (emphasis in original).

[5] *Ibid* at 62 (emphasis in original); and see Atiyah's examples, there.

[6] (1936) 46 *Yale Law Journal* 52, at 373; and see Friedmann, above n 1, at 636.

[7] 'Contract Law, Default Rules, and the Philosophy of Promising' (1989) 88 *Michigan Law Review* 489.

of 'contract as promise' theories on problems of default rules. Craswell's choice of target makes an examination of his argument particularly pertinent for our purposes.

Craswell's starting point is the perfectly acceptable notion that different theories of promissory and contractual obligation may be more or less valuable for the task of selecting default rules. Indeed, whereas one theory may have direct implications for questions of remedies, for example, another may be mostly or wholly neutral in this respect. He then argues that the latter is precisely the case with certain kinds of 'contract as promise' theory, or, more accurately, with 'contract as promise' theories which rest on certain kinds of philosophical explanation of promissory obligation. Thus he boldly asserts that 'theories which justify the binding force of promises on the basis of the obligation to tell the truth, or on considerations of individual liberty and autonomy, are of no help at all in such an enterprise.'[8]

Demonstrating this claim with regard to autonomy-based theories, Craswell concentrates on Charles Fried's, and in particular on Fried's conviction that his explanation of the binding force of promises—and therefore, for him, of contracts—*entails* that the appropriate remedy for breach is expectation damages. Fried's theory is, in this respect, but representative of a more general trend. Liberal theories of contract (or what is commonly understood as such), and more generally theories of 'contract as promise' where promises are taken to be binding,[9] tend to suggest that expectation damages (and sometimes specific performance[10]) should be the standard remedy for breach. As Atiyah put it, '[t]he liberal finds the entitlement of the promisee to the full value of the promised performance—the right to expectation damages—to be a natural corollary of basing the law on the promise principle.'[11] By referring to expectation as 'a normal and natural measure for contract damages,' however, Fried marks himself out as a particularly emphatic ambassador of this trend.[12] This would be a good juncture at which to join the debate.

Fried's argument for expectation damages as the standard remedy draws on this simple intuition:

> If I make a promise to you, I should do as I promise; and if I fail to keep my promise, it is fair that I should be made to hand over the equivalent of the promised performance.[13]

---

[8] 'Contract Law, Default Rules, and the Philosophy of Promising' (1989) 88 *Michigan Law Review* at 511.

[9] Distinguished from a view such as Atiyah's in *Promises, Morals, and Law* (Oxford, 1981), according to which contracts are promises but neither is a source of obligation.

[10] For example, Friedmann, above n 1. I return to the competition between the main performance remedies, namely specific performance and expectation (or 'performance') damages, later on in this chapter.

[11] See above n 4, Essay 6: 'The Liberal Theory of Contract,' 121, at 123.

[12] *Contract as Promise: A Theory of Contractual Obligation* (Cambridge, Massachusetts, 1981), 21.

[13] *Ibid* at 17.

and is supplemented by this simple consideration:

> The expectation standard gives the victim of a breach no more or less than he would have had had there been no breach—in other words, he gets the benefit of his bargain.[14]

But Craswell would have none of this. While conceding that concern for personal autonomy may require that people are able to undertake obligations and thus make non-optional a course of conduct that would otherwise be optional, he contends that:

> almost any remedy—reliance damages, punitive damages, specific performance, etc— makes the promised course of conduct non-optional to some degree, depending on the severity of the threatened penalty. There is surely nothing in the idea of individual autonomy that requires the exact degree of non-optionality provided by the expectation measure. . . . [N]othing in the notion of individual autonomy gives any reason for favoring the expectation measure over any of the others.[15]

Craswell concludes that since all remedies are 'equally compatible' with the notion of individual autonomy, selecting a standard remedy must involve the invocation of 'some other value'—other, that is, than that (or those) which serves to justify the binding force of promises in the first place or which follows from such a justification.[16]

It should be conceded that 'other values' may have some role to play in selecting a standard remedy. Some moral considerations which are independent from the justification for the binding force of promises (or contracts, or both), for instance, or considerations of economic efficiency which are similarly independent, may be shown to have some bearing on the matter, and if they point in directions different from those in which the 'internal' values or the theory from which they emanate point, the conflicting values would probably have to be weighed against each other before a conclusion could be reached. The question, however, is whether it is indeed the case that the underlying theory of the practice has no bearing *at all* on the question of remedies. Is it really the case that every conceivable remedy is equally compatible with this theory?

A simple counter-argument could be developed along the following lines. If a promise is binding, it invariably creates an entitlement in the promisee. And some remedies protect this entitlement better than others. Thus expectation damages, as Fried could point out, provide stronger protection for this entitlement than, say, reliance damages, for their award does not depend on the contingency of expenditure in reliance, and their monetary value would often be greater. Is this not a valid (albeit not necessarily conclusive) reason for favouring the expectation measure over the reliance one?

---

[14] *Ibid.*
[15] Above n 7, at 518.
[16] *Ibid* at 518–20.

Craswell could object by pointing out that amputation for contract-breakers would probably provide an even stronger protection for the entitlement in question, which is hardly a convincing argument for favouring it over expectation damages. But Fried has an answer for this. It is in the 'no more or less' consideration that I quoted earlier, and which Craswell conspicuously ignores. This consideration seems to indicate that there is indeed some natural continuity between acknowledging the binding force of an obligation and specifying expectation damages as the remedy for its breach—a continuity which is apparently broken when other remedies are specified, namely remedies which amount to giving the innocent party either more or less than she would have had, had there been no breach, or, to put it simply, remedies which do not reflect faithfully the value of her entitlement.

Such an argument could be further refined and further developed. For instance, as a direct reply to Craswell's claim that 'almost any remedy . . . makes the promised course of conduct non-optional to some degree,' it could be said that the variation at stake is not in terms of the degree to which a given course of conduct is made non-optional, but rather in terms of what course of conduct exactly is made non-optional (or less optional, really); and accordingly, that the expectation measure, as one that reflects the value of the entitlement which is created by a promise, no more or less, makes non-optional the promised course of conduct, no more or less, whereas the reliance measure, for instance, makes non-optional a completely different course of conduct.[17]

Here it could be pointed out that, for such an argument to work, it need not really matter *why* promises (or contracts, for that matter) are held to be binding: it only matters that they are. Later I will illustrate how the reasons for which contracts are held to be binding do have an important bearing on the choice of standard remedy. But even regardless of that, the case is clearly different from one where the underlying theory of the practice is wholly irrelevant for the question of remedies, as Craswell contends. Accordingly, those 'other values' the role of which Craswell highlights may come into play at a logically secondary juncture, and in a much less open-ended way than he envisages: the question would be whether some other values—other than those which justify the practice itself and the core rights and obligations which it is meant to recognise or create, or which follow from such justification—entail that expectation damages (or, as we shall see, specific performance) should *not* be the standard remedy for breach.

---

[17] In the case of reliance damages, this course of conduct is something like 'compensating the promisee if, and only if, she suffers a loss as a result of reasonably relying on a promise which was later broken, and compensating her for, and only for, this loss.' An argument along similar lines was presented by Friedmann in his convincing reply to Fuller and Perdue. See above n 1, especially at 635–38.

Choosing a Performance Remedy: Why Not Specific Performance?

Let us stay for the moment with the Fried-Craswell debate. Victory thus far, I suggested, belongs to Fried: succinct though his argument is, it contains enough to rebuff Craswell's sweeping claim that a theory of contractual obligation such as Fried's is 'of no help at all' for the enterprise of choosing a standard remedy for breach of contract, and more specifically that it provides nothing in the shape of 'any reason for favoring the expectation measure over any of the others.' But is Fried's argument ultimately successful?

As we have seen, Fried's argument succeeds in showing that the expectation measure of damages enjoys theoretical support over, among others, reliance damages, because it reflects the very value of contractual performance (and, with this in mind, I will occasionally refer to it as a 'performance' remedy). However expectation damages are not the only performance remedy. Another is, of course, actual enforcement of the contract, by way of ordering specific performance (or its practical equivalent, an injunction against breach). And here lies the problem. In arguing for expectation damages Fried completely ignores the option of specific performance, while his succinct argument in no way explains this surprising omission. On the contrary: when he writes that '[i]f I make a promise to you, I should do as I promise; and if I fail to keep my promise, it is fair that I should be made to hand over the equivalent of the promised performance,' his narrative only begs the question why not drop the 'equivalent of' bit; and when he commends expectation damages for giving the victim of a breach 'no more or less than he would have had had there been no breach—in other words . . . the benefit of his bargain,' specific performance springs to mind as something which, when applicable, could surely achieve this very aim more simply, more directly, and more accurately. After all, specific performance is the remedy that aims at granting the innocent party precisely what she bargained for, whereas expectation damages merely aim at compensating her, albeit fully, for not receiving what she bargained for. At best, excuse the pun, it is a second best. So why not opt for the best?

Fried's neglect of specific performance is particularly surprising given that for him, as he put it, 'a contract is first of all a promise,' so that 'the contract must be kept because a promise must be kept.'[18] The core contractual obligation, in other words, is not different from the core promissory obligation: it is an obligation to perform. But of course this view is not unique to Fried: it is shared by many a theoretician, practitioner and lay person. I would speculate that, despite the emergence of arguments suggesting otherwise, it is still the most prevalent approach to the nature of contract and the normative foundations of contract law. Moreover, the emergence of arguments suggesting otherwise, by scholars as disparate as OW Holmes and Grant Gilmore, has been largely inspired by the

---

[18] Above n 12, at 17.

very fact that specific performance is not the standard or most common response to a breach of contract. The traditional prominence at common law of expectation damages and the relative rarity of actual enforcement has always provided ammunition to those who argue that contract law does not recognise and is not based upon an obligation to perform and a right to performance, but rather on some tort-like obligation to compensate for non-performance and its corresponding right.

Whereas Fried ignored the problem, some who share his view that the core contractual obligation and the core contractual right are performance of the contract have offered various explanations for the apparent discrepancy between this view and familiar regimes of remedies for breach. These explanation, as I will now suggest, have mostly been unsuccessful, or at least incomplete.

To start, it may be worth noting that explanations in terms of alluding to the historical origins of the competing remedies could not suffice. Contract law textbooks routinely point out that whereas the award of damages has always been a common law measure, specific performance originally emerged as an equitable remedy, hence its discretionary status in English law today. But this, obviously, is not a principled explanation for the law today, let alone that even within the artificial boundaries that it draws, the problem is bound to resurface: once courts have the discretion to order specific performance, why exercise this discretion so sparingly? What guidelines should courts be provided with for its exercise, and on what normative basis?

Another familiar suggestion, this time one which is at least aimed at normative foundations, rests on the notion that specific performance is intrinsically harsh. A similar suggestion, perhaps a more specific iteration of the same idea, is the notion that specific performance represents an excessive interference with personal freedom.[19] I think that these explanations point us in the right direction. (Indeed, the solution that I will introduce later follows a similar orientation.) But they are invariably incomplete. The alleged harshness of specific performance is by no means obvious or self-explanatory. It may be so in some specific cases or classes of case, due to the more or less exceptional nature of the contractual relations or the circumstances of the contractual dispute at stake,[20] but not in general. Often an order of specific performance would amount to no more than forcing the party in breach to sell something or buy something or render some service on a none-too-personal, one-off basis, and such like. If such treatment is harsh, it is not evident why. And it is a similar case with the notion of 'excessive' interference with personal freedom. 'Excessive' is a normative term, and judging an action to amount to excessive interference with a person's

---

[19] See eg AT Kronman, 'Paternalism and the Law of Contracts' (1983) 92 *Yale Law Journal* 763, at 778–79; J Penner, 'Voluntary Obligations and the Scope of the Law of Contract' (1996) 2 *Legal Theory* 325, at 353.

[20] A striking illustration of the kind of special case I have in mind here is *Patel v Ali* [1984] Ch 283, where specific performance, in a contractual area where it is normally available, was refused due to a disastrous change in the seller's circumstances subsequent to the signing of the contract.

freedom can only be an evaluative, not a factual, judgement. And as such, again, it is far from self-explanatory in the present context. After all, specific performance is merely intended to make a person discharge an obligation that she undertook, herself, voluntarily. Of course the excess, like harshness, may be quite straightforward to ascertain in particular cases where, for instance, a change of circumstances means that performing a previously undertaken obligation *now* would involve giving up some once-in-a-lifetime opportunity or making some other, extraordinary sacrifice. But such cases can at best (can very probably) justify an exception; as an evaluative matter, it remains to be seen whether concern for personal freedom counsels against the adoption of specific performance as a rule.

A different and very interesting argument was offered recently by Steve Smith.[21] Smith's argument is particularly interesting for present purposes, because it draws directly not only on the notion that contractual obligations are binding, but on (some of) the reasons for holding them to be so. It draws, in other words, on what Craswell would label 'a philosophical theory' of contract. Moreover, the theory in question is of the particular kind that Craswell specifies as strictly unhelpful: it rests on considerations of 'individual liberty and autonomy.' Though I shall soon argue that Smith's argument is ultimately unsuccessful, my refutation of it will follow a similar path and draw on similar sources. I will outline my reasons for thinking not that Smith was wrong to seek a link between the theory explaining the source of substantive rights and obligations on the one hand and the choice of standard remedy on the other, but (mainly) that his argument hinges on an erroneous understanding of a certain aspect of the nature of contract. If nothing else, this will complete the thus-far only partial rejection of Craswell's view.

Having rejected (for reasons similar to mine) some traditional explanations for the law's reluctance to grant specific performance (as well as to punish a deliberate breach of contract),[22] Smith's own argument turns on what he calls the 'bond-creating' function of contract. 'Contracts are,' he writes, 'first of all, promises, and keeping promises is one of the most important ways that individuals develop bonds with each other.'[23] Thus a breach of contract can cause, alongside what he calls 'the tangible harm' (that is, the innocent party's failure to receive that for which it bargained) another kind of harm, this time 'intangible': 'A breach prevents the creation of—or, in the case of deliberate breach, destroys—the bonds that were developing between the contracting parties.'[24] Now whereas the award of no remedy could ever redress the intangible harm caused by a breach, the routine availability of specific performance 'would make

[21] SA Smith, 'Performance, Punishment and the Nature of Contractual Obligation' (1997) 60 *Modern Law Review* 360.

[22] *Ibid* at 363–64.

[23] *Ibid* at 369.

[24] *Ibid*.

the intangible benefits of contracting more difficult to achieve.'[25] By obscuring parties' motives for performance—since the known, general availability of specific performance would prevent parties from *knowing* 'whether or not performance has been done for the right reasons' and even 'make it *less likely*' that this is the case[26]—it would deprive performance, and hence contracting in general, of much of its bond-creating potential, thus 'making the valuable activity of contracting less valuable.'[27] Preferring damages to specific performance as the standard remedy for breach is thus justified as a way of leaving more scope 'for the operation of good intentions.'[28]

At first blush the argument looks attractive, especially given that Smith tackles elegantly what is probably the most obvious objection, namely the notion that the alleged bond-creating function of the practice would be seriously undermined not only by the general availability of specific performance but by any kind of institutionalised, well-advertised, and efficient regime of remedies, even one that does not opt routinely for the most stringent way of protecting contractual entitlements. In other words, it could be argued that taking the bond-creating function of contract seriously entails not only passing over the choice of specific performance for standard remedy, but perhaps limiting legal protection to discretionary intervention in relatively extreme cases of loss suffered in reliance, and no more. Conceding that the elimination of all remedies would indeed 'make performance an even stronger affirmation of the special ties binding contracting parties,' Smith points out that whereas specific performance is a wholly ineffective means of rectifying the intangible harm caused by a breach, monetary damages remain independently justifiable as an effective means of rectifying the tangible harm, so that, on the balance of considerations, their elimination is not called for after all.[29]

Yet by now it should be clear why I would ultimately reject Smith's argument. I said earlier that it hinges on an erroneous understanding of a certain aspect of the nature of contract, and what I had in mind is of course the very attribution of a bond-creating function to this practice. In Smith's case this is palpably the upshot of following the well-established theoretical tradition of likening contract to promise (remember the starting point: 'Contracts are, first of all, promises'), here manifesting itself with particular force by the unquestioning and un-argued-for assumption that contract and promise must share all their functions and values. By contrast, the differences between contract and promise that I highlighted in previous chapters suggest that whereas the intrinsic function and value of promise are at odds with the notion of enforced performance—indeed, at odds for the very reason Smith outlined, having erroneously

[25] SA Smith, 'Performance, Punishment and the Nature of Contractual Obligation' (1997) 60 *Modern Law Review* at 370.

[26] *Ibid* at 370–71 (emphasis added).

[27] *Ibid* at 371.

[28] *Ibid*.

[29] *Ibid*.

attributed to contract the same function and value—nothing about the nature of contract produces similar conclusions. The symbolic (or 'expressive') significance of a promise, the element which gives it its special value and its relationship-enhancing potential, is ruined anyway when a promise is enforced. Even the mere prospect of enforcement could seriously undermine a promise's potential to promote personal relationships, because it interferes with the necessary transparency of motives. In contract, where the parties are often strangers, where the significance of performance is typically independent of motives, and where parties are likely to be ignorant of and indifferent to their counterparts' motives anyway, such considerations simply do not apply.[30]

With this objection to specific performance removed, it is back in contention as the remedy that best supports the practice's instrumental function. Not only is it back in contention, but the case for specific performance now emerges with greater force, for the routine availability of this remedy would also be conducive to the promotion of the intrinsic value that the practice does possess, and to the operation of the intrinsic function that it is far more adept at fulfilling and far more commonly expected to fulfil: that of facilitating personal detachment. For as far as personal detachment is concerned, the less scope left for 'the operation of good intentions' the better. To put it less provocatively, the greater the extent to which the practice can guarantee that participants would achieve through contracting precisely what they hoped to achieve in entering the contract, with minimal hassle and minimal anxiety, the better the practice at enabling participants to deal with others without being *reliant* on personal relations, and while maintaining, if they so wish, their personal detachment.

So the search for an explanation for the law's reluctance to award specific performance is still on. In the next section I will introduce my proposed solution. As I hinted earlier, this solution is meant to substantiate the claim that the main or most common reason to opt for the award of damages instead is that specific performance represents an excessive interference with personal freedom. But what often renders specific performance excessive is not some intrinsic, self-explanatory harshness. It can only be judged excessive by reference to the (legitimate) purposes for which participants engage in the practice in the first place,

---

[30] Here I may be reminded that earlier I accepted Smith's contention that insisting on the elimination of specific performance in order not to interfere with the alleged bond-creating function of contract need not be accompanied by a call for the elimination of all other remedies. Does this concession on my part call my very argument concerning the intrinsic function and value of contract into question? It might be thought so, since in making that argument I drew, inter alia, on the typical availability of remedies for breach, but not necessarily specific performance. But the context makes all the difference. What I accepted when introducing Smith's argument was the notion that, *assuming that the practice really has, in common with the practice of promise, a bond-creating function,* then more scope would be left for this function to operate by the removal of specific performance (or, similarly, punitive damages) even if (certain) other remedies remain available. My argument overall, by contrast, was aimed at rebuffing the very notion that a bond-creating function should be attributed to contract in the first place—an argument that can indeed draw on the inevitable implications of familiar remedial regimes, regardless of whether or not these designate specific performance as a standard remedy or make it routinely available.

in conjunction with some independently valid principle of freedom. The principle I have in mind can be perceived as an entailment or interpretation of a principle which is widely accepted as governing much broader aspects of our legal and political structures. It is the harm principle.

The Harm Principle and Remedies for Breach

What kind of a solution is my proposed solution going to be? A suspicion which may arise at this stage is that the case built for specific performance in the previous section would now prove too robust to be demolished, especially so once we are reminded of the nature of the task at hand, namely to find grounds for a mere starting point for considering remedies—to find grounds for a general rule—while bearing in mind that instances where deviation from the rule could be justified may indeed be many. Is what has been said thus far not enough to establish specific performance as this starting point or general rule?

In fact, I think it is enough. And if so, then all that is left for the proposed solution to explain is, indeed, what is perceived as a widespread reluctance, in the form of awarding damages, to follow that rule—or, if you want, the familiar willingness to make exceptions—and not just in contractual disputes whose circumstances are exceptional or in particular categories of contract where specific performance is impractical or particularly harsh. But since now the role reserved for the proposed solution may (though I doubt that it should) appear to be less ambitious, I should at this juncture mention that a more careful examination of legal practice suggests that the explanatory task is in fact not quite as demanding as it may have appeared to be in the first place. A remedy for breach that has been much neglected in theoretical discussions of the subject is 'action for debt' (or 'action for an agreed sum'). The reason for this neglect may well be the fact that little is usually said about this remedy in textbooks, as well as in high-level judicial decisions. But this, far from being an indication of the relative practical insignificance of action for debt, can be explained by the fact that this rather straightforward remedy (and the rather straightforward legal action which usually brings it about) has given rise to little in the way of practical or doctrinal difficulty. Action for debt is, however, one of the most common (if not *the* most common) legal actions brought in the aftermath or in the face of a breach of contract, and the rather routine award of an order of payment in such actions must not be confused with the award of damages. In an action for debt the plaintiff does not sue for compensation for loss suffered as a result of a breach, but rather for the very performance of the defendant's primary contractual obligation—performance that in this case happens to be the payment of monies.[31]

---

[31] For a discussion, see eg GH Treitel, *The Law of Contract* (10th edn, London, 1999) 943–49. (For an illustration of the point made in the text, note that here action for debt receives six pages of discussion, and this in a 127 pages-long chapter on remedies.)

The discussion in the previous section established specific performance as the general rule, as it showed it to be the most robust and most straightforward way of serving both the instrumental and the intrinsic functions of contract law. But that discussion also holds the key to the most prevalent justification for deviating from the rule. For it showed the value of performance for parties to contract to be typically isolated from all other aspects of their transaction or interaction. The value of the contract's subject matter for the innocent party, its value as a bargain, is typically all that needs to be guaranteed—all that there is to be protected—in order for parties to achieve through contracting precisely what they hoped to achieve in the first place. And this means that in the ordinary commercial context, where the whole purpose of the transaction is to facilitate some future profit, as well as very often in non-commercial contracts (where the purpose of the contract is similar, or where its subject matter is some truly generic commodity, etc), expectation damages, though a substitutionary remedy in their rationale, are simply just as good.

Let me reiterate this point with another glance at the comparison between contract and promise. It might seem strange for me to say that whereas promissory performance often has additional value for the promisee over and above its immediate instrumental value the same is not true of contractual performance, for after all I have argued that as a practice contract, too, possesses value over and above its instrumental one. But the contrast between the respective intrinsic values of the two practices explains this. Unlike personal relationships, personal detachment is something that only has a distinct value and only requires protection or support where and inasmuch as it is endangered. Contracts support personal detachment by removing a potential source of dependence on pre-existing relationships. This does not make contractual performance valuable in a way that transcends its value as part of a bargain, for detachment between parties who are only brought into contact in the context of the bargain does not have any distinct value and is not something that requires protection outside of this very context. On the contrary: making it the case that the value of a contract or of contractual performance for a party is no more and no less than its instrumental value, its value as a bargain or as part of a bargain, is exactly what promoting personal detachment in this context is all about. It is about the ability to make a reliable deal with another party without necessarily bringing much else into it, *so that* the value of the exchange is its value per se, its value as a bargain, and performance is valuable simply as part of that bargain, as something that is necessary in order to bring a beneficial transaction to completion.

The same can be seen if we concentrate not on the value of performance but on the potential harm caused through a failure to perform. In promise, this harm would often exceed the losses, if any, which are related directly to the failure to receive the thing promised. A broken promise can be a missed opportunity to enhance personal relationships. Moreover promise-making, as we have seen, typically involves the invocation of personal trust so that an unjustified breach—the abuse of this trust—amounts to an insult to the promisee, a failure to treat her as a person.[32] This, in turn, can shatter relationships, and not only represent a missed opportunity to bolster them. Contractual relations, by contrast, typically do not (indeed, typically *cannot*) depend on personal trust in the same sense and to the same extent as promissory relations, and making a contract need not involve the invocation of personal trust the same way promise-making typically does.[33] Thus in breach of contract, considerations of abused trust and personal insult are simply not an issue the way they often are in promise-breaking. When such a breach occurs, the harm, if any, is simply in terms of losing the benefits of the bargain. And as long as the harm in these terms is redressed, the ability to deal with others while maintaining personal detachment is secured: the breach itself, that is regardless of its harmful effect in terms of the expected benefits of the transaction, cannot undermine it in any way.

All this still does not answer the question as to why the law should allow the party in breach to choose whether to perform or to compensate for non-performance, even in those cases where choosing the latter would leave the innocent party equally well-off. This is where the required principle of freedom must come into play. In light of what has been just established in the preceding paragraphs, however, perhaps all that is needed is, to use Joel Feinberg's language, 'a general presumption in favour of liberty.'[34] Given that specific performance is a more intrusive remedy than damages—at any rate, that enforced performance amounts to a greater interference with personal freedom compared to allowing the party in breach to *choose* between performance and compensation for non-performance—such a simple presumption suffices to recommend the latter in all those cases where the innocent party (and hence, plausibly, the practice of contract) would not in any way be worse-off as a result.

It could be argued in response that the scope for making that presumption in favour of liberty (that is, let us not forget, in favour of the liberty of the party *in breach*) is not that obvious. After all, the breaching party's obligation to its counterpart was assumed voluntarily (and, *ex hypothesi*, effectively) by it in the first place, and the obligation was an obligation to perform rather than an obligation to choose between performance and compensation come performance time. In morality, at least, this party's freedom so to choose is far from evident. But the question here is not the nature of the moral obligation; rather, it has to do with considerations of personal freedom in the legal imposition of (remedial) obligations. And in this context, the invocation of a principle of freedom, potentially 'in favour' of those who fail morally, is familiar and broadly accepted. Indeed, the argument can be introduced as an interpretation or an implication of the harm principle.

---

[32] See Chapter 1 on what is wrong with breaking a promise.
[33] See Chapter 3 on enforceability and the trivialisation of the role of trust.
[34] J Feinberg, *Harm to Others* (Oxford, 1984) 9.

According to a possible formulation of the harm principle, the imposition of legal obligations on individuals is justified only when done in order to prevent or redress harm. Given the routine allusion to various versions of this principle in numerous other areas of legal and political discussion, it is perhaps a little surprising to find that its invocation in discussions of remedies for breach of contract has been exceedingly rare. A possible explanation for the reluctance to allude to the harm principle in this context, even by scholars from the liberal tradition, is that taken at face value, the principle seems incapable of settling the competition between legal measures such as specific performance and expectation damages, because they are both designed to redress or prevent precisely the same harm, namely loss of bargain. If so, then if the harm principle bestows legitimacy on one remedy, it would legitimate the use of the other just the same. It could not, in other words, in any way settle or shed light on the internal competition between them.

This view is supported by the Millian formulation of the harm principle. In Mill's canonical defence of such a principle, the principle sets a necessary condition of justified restraint of liberty, but says nothing as to what measures ought to be taken when this condition (and possibly others) is satisfied. (As John Gray put it, 'the principle [does not] tell us how much liberty may be restrained for the sake of the prevention of how much harm. As far as the [principle] itself is concerned, a severe restriction of liberty could be imposed for the sake of the prevention of a minor harm.'[35]) In Mill's case, this limitation on the applicability of the harm principle is probably the result of the somewhat tenuous relations between utilitarianism and the doctrine of liberty in his moral and political thought. A particularly powerful interpretation of the harm principle that is unaffected by such concerns is Joseph Raz's.[36] Raz has shown how (a version of) the harm principle can be vindicated from the perspective of a moral theory that sees the key to political freedom in the value of personal autonomy, and how, defended and reinterpreted as such, the harm principle can serve as a far richer source of inspiration for and scrutiny of legal policy than its common understanding as 'setting a necessary condition for the justification of coercion and nothing more.'[37]

My suggestion as to how the harm principle can be brought to bear on the contest between specific performance and expectation damages is simple. Though it is only from the perspective of a substantive theory of political freedom that the harm principle can be defended and given concrete content, the very fact that it is a principle of restraint reflecting concern for personal freedom renders it a rather straightforward implication of (any satisfactory interpretation of) this principle that whenever a certain harm could be effectively prevented in more

---

[35] JS Mill, *On Liberty and Other Essays* (Oxford World's Classics edn, Oxford, 1998), Introduction, xix. See also J Gray, *Mill on Liberty: A Defence* (2nd edn, London, 1996), and D Lyons, *Rights, Welfare, and Mill's Moral Theory* (Oxford, 1994), especially ch. 4.

[36] See *The Morality of Freedom* (Oxford, 1986) especially ch 15.

[37] *Ibid* at 421.

that one way, the measure that must be used is the least intrusive one—the measure that, compared to its alternatives, amounts to a lesser interference with the freedom of the person against whom it is taken. Thus when it comes to remedies for breach of contract, the harm principle, assuming that it is compatible in the first place with the imposition of legal obligations in order to prevent or redress the harm which is loss of bargain, counsels against the employment of the more intrusive remedy whenever the award of a less intrusive remedy could redress this harm just as effectively. More specifically, the upshot is that even if it is thought that the plaintiff's 'core' right is the right to performance, accepting the harm principle entails that specific performance should be awarded only when the less intrusive remedial measure, the award of (expectation) damages, could not fully redress the harm caused through a violation of this right.

Employing the logic and language of the harm principle in this context is particularly useful as it serves to remind us of two key points. First, that denying the innocent party of specific performance need not amount to denying that the party in breach should have performed in the first place: the very point of the harm principle is to suggest that something more than a mere failure to do what is right may be required in order to justify legal enforcement.[38] Secondly, that special reasons against the award of specific performance may prevail even in circumstances where the harm principle requirement is satisfied: that is, the harm principle is but a negative guideline—while providing that the imposition of legal obligations is justified only when done in order to prevent or redress harm, it does not entail that obligations should be imposed in order to prevent every harm or redress it to the full, and does not purport to exclude special reasons for not doing so where such reasons exist. Thus in those particular cases or categories of case with which contract lawyers are familiar, where considerations such as the spectre of economic waste on a grand scale, the inherent difficulty in supervising performance, or the exceptional hardship that enforced performance would cause militate against the award of specific performance, opting for a 'lesser' remedy may be justified even though the innocent party's (otherwise) legitimate interest in performance is not in doubt.

I said earlier that it has been exceedingly rare for the harm principle to be invoked in discussions of remedies for breach of contract. I am, in fact, aware of one such case, and that is Raz's own deployment of the harm principle in such a context. But unlike my argument, which alludes to the harm principle as a possible justification for deviating from the rule which is specific performance,

---

[38] Indeed, it is far from clear to me that morally speaking, at least, the obligation to perform automatically evaporates (or is being transformed into something else) even in circumstances where compensation for non-performance would leave the innocent party equally well-off. If anything, the analogy to promise seems to suggest otherwise, since in such circumstances it is probably still down to the promisee to release the promisor from her original obligation. This may remain the case even if in the circumstances it happens to be the promisee's *duty* to grant this release. Such a duty, it should be noted, may be one that arises not directly out of the promise or promissory logic, but rather out of the background relationship between promisor and promisee—it could, for instance, be a special duty arising out of friendship. For another example of this possibility see below n 47.

Raz's suggests that the harm principle supports a remedial regime whereby none of the performance remedies is the rule. Allow me to quote his concise argument in its entirety:

> Those who, like myself, accept Mill's harm principle or some modified version of it will doubt the legitimacy of the law's adoption of a general policy of enforcing voluntary obligations. . . . It follows from the harm principle that enforcing voluntary obligations is not itself a proper goal for contract law. To enforce voluntary obligations is to enforce morality through the legal imposition of duties on individuals. In this respect it does not differ from the legal proscription of pornography. Compensating individuals for harm resulting from reliance on voluntary obligations is, on the other hand, a proper goal for the law. As far as this argument goes, supporters of the harm principle should favour reliance damages rather than expectation damages as a standard legal remedy for breach of contract. Contrary to often expressed views, the belief that the proper role of contract law is the protection of the practice of undertaking voluntary obligations does not necessarily lead to endorsement of an expectation-value measure of the legal protection of contracts.[39]

As a professed supporter of the harm principle (and, moreover, of the same version of the principle adopted by Raz), I should explain why I do not think that the principle lends support, not even prima facie, to limiting remedial intervention to compensation for loss incurred in reliance. But before I do so, it should be noted that although the emphasis in my argument thus far has been on how the harm principle can legitimise the transition from specific performance to expectation damages (as this is bound to be the most prevalent scenario), the same argument indicates how sometimes the harm principle would support the imposition of a lesser remedial obligation still, such as reliance damages, and sometimes not even that. To take the extreme case, in cases where, say, a buyer reneges but an alternative buyer is ready to step in under the same conditions (price, schedule, etc), and the circumstances are such that the new transaction is entirely costless for the seller (and no loss of 'transaction volume' is at issue, etc), the harm principle as I deployed it would counsel against the award of any remedy against the original buyer. Or if the case is similar other than the fact that the seller has already incurred some expense in reliance on the original buyer's performance, then my argument would support reliance damages but no more. But my position still is very different from Raz's, as according to his argument the harm principle is incompatible with expectation damages (let alone specific performance) even in cases where the award of the lesser remedy would not suffice to put the innocent party in just as good a position as that in which it would have been had the contract been performed.

Unlike my proposed solution, Raz's view is, to my mind, simply incompatible with holding the core contractual obligation to be an obligation to perform and the core contractual right a right to performance—a proposition that Raz himself did not seek to deny as a basis for his argument concerning remedies. Raz's

[39] Above n 2, at 934.

view on the harm principle's implications in terms of remedies for breach depends for its validity on the notion that denying the innocent party the benefits of the bargain through an unjustified breach does not amount to harming it (not for the purposes of the harm principle, at any rate). But if the innocent party's core contractual right is the right to performance, and so a right to the advantages or benefits that performance would bring about, then this view is unsustainable. 'Harm' is a forward-looking concept. To harm a person is to affect adversely her prospects, deny her of what she is entitled to, and the like. And if the benefits of the bargain are something to which parties to contract are entitled—part and parcel of seeing them as the subject of the parties' core rights—then at least inasmuch as these benefits are of a discernible value for a party, denying them to this party is harming it, and harming it in a rather paradigmatic sense. The fact that the innocent party had not yet had, prior to the breach or indeed prior to the formation of the contract, the very benefits (profit, etc) that it was denied through the breach (as opposed to, say, the money it lost through reasonable expenditure in reliance) simply does not matter. The fact that an aspiring concert pianist has not yet enjoyed the fame and the income that her talent would undoubtedly have brought her had her hands not been damaged irreversibly does not mean that such lost prospects are not a component of the harm done to her through the damaging of her hands. The harm principle is equally compatible with a general policy of awarding performance remedies for breach of contract as it is with legal measures designed to prevent or redress (among other things) the loss of future income by the injured pianist.[40]

Raz's argument concerning the implications of the harm principle for remedies was followed by three considerations which, he conceded, could tilt the balance in favour of performance remedies after all. It should be instructive to consider them briefly in turn. The first is a practical consideration of legal

---

[40] We can now see where the analogy Raz draws between the legal enforcement of voluntary obligations and the legal proscription of pornography falls apart. To follow the analogy we have to assume that performed contracts and a pornography-free environment are both, morally speaking, good things. But here lies the difference. Parties to contracts' right to performance—their moral right, at any rate—can be traced to obligations voluntarily and effectively assumed by their counterparts. This is the view shared by Raz and me. The question as to whether or not people (in general, or women in particular) have a right to a pornography-free environment, by contrast, is at the very centre of the debate concerning the proscription of pornography. Raz (as his use of this example attests) and many others think that though a pornography-free world might be a good thing indeed, preventing this good from materialising does not amount to harming anybody, and is hence incompatible with the harm principle. Arguments in support of the proscription of pornography typically seek to establish that pornography, over and above being morally repugnant, in fact harms (certain) people, directly and seriously, for instance, by encouraging sexual aggression towards women, so that its proscription becomes something to which people are entitled (and so that, in turn, a failure to do so may again amount to harming, or at any rate that proscribing pornography is not incompatible with the harm principle). It is the very existence of such an entitlement that the objectors deny. Note that in a later text, Raz wrote the following: 'Roughly speaking, one harms another when one's action makes the other person worse off than he was, *or is entitled to be*, in a way which affects his future well-being' (above n 36, at 414; emphasis added.) This view strikes me as incompatible with his earlier argument concerning the harm principle and remedies for breach.

policy: 'to leave it to the courts to determine in every case whether reliance on the contract caused harm would lead to expensive litigation and frequent judicial mistakes.'[41] This may well be so, but I doubt that it could count as sufficient reason to make expectation damages (or, for that matter, specific performance) the standard remedy. The likelihood of judicial mistakes and the prospect of expensive litigation notwithstanding, we may prefer to take the risk (and perhaps try to minimise it by other means, such as through the rules governing evidence and procedure) rather than opt for a solution by which parties are systematically subjected to remedial duties even though they caused no harm (or caused harm of much smaller magnitude).

The second consideration has to do with the notion that 'the frustration of expectations may itself cause harm for which the law may seek to compensate.'[42] While I do not disagree with this either, I do not think that this consideration really leaves an open door for expectation damages (or again, specific performance). Not wide open enough, at any rate, for even in cases where an emotional harm caused by frustration can clearly be identified (and identified or quantified as exceeding the applicable reliance measure of damages) expectation damages need not emerge as the correct measure. Putting a price on frustration is of course not easy, but it would plainly be arbitrary to assume that the price is always identical to the value of performance. It may be more and it may be less. It would depend, in a given case, on the psychological makeup of the injured party (when it is a person) and on numerous other aspects, financial, for instance, of its current situation (even when it is not a person), and of course on the actual value of performance in the particular case. In short, the unfortunate label 'expectation damages'[43] by no means guarantees a correlation between the measure of damages it denotes and the actual value of frustrated expectations.

The third consideration is as follows: 'Since protecting the practice of undertaking voluntary obligations from erosion and debasement prevents harm, enforcement of contracts can be accepted if justified as a means to that end.'[44] This is an important reminder of the fact that remedies for breach, other than protecting contracting parties, have an additional function: that of protecting the practice itself. For supporters of the harm principle, the legitimacy of this function, too, depends on accepting a certain version of the harm principle: a version that accommodates (and so allows for measures designed to prevent) institutional harm. Though as I indicated earlier the two legitimate functions of remedies are closely related, Raz alludes to this second function to illustrate how the protection of the practice could justify the legal imposition of (remedial) obligations even where the protection of individual participants in the practice does not. Now unlike Raz, I argued that the protection of contracting parties against harm does, in principle, warrant resort to performance remedies.

---

[41] Above n 2, at 937.
[42] *Ibid* at 937–38.
[43] See Friedmann, above n 1, at 633–34.
[44] Above n 2, 937.

Nevertheless, the case for these can be reinforced by a separate examination of what is involved in the protection of the practice. I wish to conclude the current discussion with two brief points on this issue.

The first point is a direct implication of the argument concerning the protection of parties to contract, and serves as an illustration of the interrelation between the two main functions of remedies. The fact that the reliance measure of damages is often inadequate, as I argued, for the task of protecting parties against harm, marks it out also as inadequate for the task of protecting the practice against erosion and debasement, as these are particularly likely to result from the practice's very failure to protect its participants. If parties remained largely unprotected against unjustified denials of the benefits for which they have engaged in the practice in the first place (that is, entered a contract) and to which they are entitled—if parties were only protected against the contingency of loss suffered in actual reliance but not otherwise—the practice of making contracts would lose much of its efficacy and much of its point.

The second point, though again related, pertains more directly to the protection of the practice as a whole. Since the reliance measure deters and compensates for a breach only when actual expenditure or loss in reliance occurred and only to the extent of such an expenditure or loss, selecting it as the standard response to breach of contract would encourage a peculiar and highly undesirable (economically and otherwise) contractual conduct: parties who are keen on performance (or, at any rate, on securing the benefits performance was to bring about) would be impelled to generate unnecessary or fictitious reliance-expenditure, whereas parties who are keen on leaving open the possibility of a future breach would try to prevent or discourage their counterparts from relying.[45] While contract, as a practice, should be expected, among other things, to enable and in the right circumstances encourage expenditure in reliance, this is not in itself its only or even main purpose. Not only the occurrence but also the desirability of expenditure in reliance is merely contingent upon a range of considerations that are inseparable from the nature and circumstances of individual transactions and the type and purpose of the expenditure itself. Creating an artificial reason to generate (or to thwart) such expenditure by making its occurrence a necessary condition for and its value a limit upon legal protection is bound to undermine the practice's ability to fulfil its main functions.

By contrast, the approach I outlined above excels as a means of protecting the practice precisely because of its sensitivity to the practice's main functions and values, sensitivity which was guaranteed through the concern for protecting participants. Specific performance as the rule serves better than any alternative rule both the practice's instrumental function and value of co-operation, and the practice's intrinsic function and value, personal detachment. And deviations from this rule, inasmuch as they are governed, as suggested, by the harm prin-

---

[45] For a similar argument see Atiyah, above n 4, Essay 7: 'Executory Contracts, Expectation Damages, and the Economic Analysis of Contract', at 170–71.

ciple, could do little to undermine the practice's propensity to fulfil these functions and promote these values. The fact that such deviations do not involve a compromise to the legitimate advantages which parties can and hope to derive from participation in the practice, coupled with the very fact that the logic that governs such deviations from the rule, prevalent as the circumstances that allow them may be, is that of making an exception (indeed, deviating from a rule), together guarantee as much.

Mitigation

The discussion of remedies for breach of contract would not be complete without a glance at two residual issues: the common law doctrine pertaining to the mitigation of damages (or the so-called 'duty' to mitigate damages), and the (supposedly valuable) freedom to change one's mind. Both deserve attention if only because they feature quite effectively in one of the most thorough and original attacks on liberal theory of contract, that offered by Patrick Atiyah.

The mitigation doctrine's claim on our attention is particularly clear, for the challenge it offers, in the shape of an apparent discrepancy between legal practice and the notion that the core contractual obligation is performance, is similar to the challenge I addressed earlier in this chapter. In fact, the new challenge might seem even greater. Where the mitigation rules apply in the aftermath of a breach of contract, the amount recoverable by the innocent party may be far less than the value of performance (whereas expectation damages are at least intended to reflect the value of performance). For this reason, Atiyah pointed out that '[a]n adequate explanation of the mitigation rule is . . . an essential part of the argument of the liberal theorist when it is suggested that the expectation damages rule follows as a natural corollary from the promise principle.'[46] Even more essential, it could be said, when unlike Fried (Atiyah's direct target in this quotation) a liberal theorist suggests that specific performance rather than expectation damages should be the standard remedy for breach.

Let us clarify the nature of the challenge posed by the mitigation doctrine. The doctrine comprises two rules: one prescribing actions designed to minimise the loss caused (or about to be caused) by a breach, the other prohibiting actions designed to exacerbate it. Now it matters little that, despite frequent references in the literature to a 'duty' to mitigate, neither rule in fact imposes a duty on the innocent party. The innocent party is not under a legal duty to minimise its losses nor to refrain from exacerbating them, but doing just that becomes very much in this party's interest given that the practical effect of the rules is to set a limit on the amount recoverable from the party in breach so that this amount would not include 'exacerbated' losses, nor losses that *could have been* mitigated. In practical terms, to put it simply, the mitigation rules makes it the case

---

[46] Above n 11, at 124.

that it is *for* the innocent party to take certain steps to minimise its losses and to refrain from taking steps that would exacerbate it. Duty or not, this is enough for the challenge to materialise.

The challenge materialises, let me make it clear, not because the so-called duty to mitigate is morally inexplicable. Far from it: in a promissory context, to take a particularly pertinent example, the mitigation rules (or something similar) can be accommodated rather easily, and perhaps even accommodated as a real duty. The problem is that in such a context, the duty to mitigate would not reflect promissory logic as such, but rather emanate from that framework of relationship in which promises are typically made. If, for instance, a friend has broken a promise she made me and I can quite straightforwardly lessen the harm I am likely to suffer as a result, not to do so and then try to hold her responsible for the resulting harm (in its entirety) would seem at odds with the very concept of friendship. Thus understood, however, mitigation is something I may owe my promisor-friend specifically as a friend. It is a requirement which coincides with or materialises through her act of promise-making—or, more accurately, promise-breaking—but which does not arise out of the promise itself nor as a direct implication of my status as a promisee.[47]

This could explain why in Fried's *Contract as Promise* (surely the most meticulous modern attempt to reconcile promissory logic with contract law reality) the mitigation rules receive what is probably the least satisfactory treatment. After all, to argue that contract law is based on promissory logic is one thing; but to argue that the law randomly imports various other, related standards of conduct that feature specifically in those frameworks of personal relationship in which promises are typically made is quite another. And viewed in isolation, the mitigation rules, with their practical effect of diminishing, albeit post-breach, the scope and the value of contractual obligations appear if anything to go against promissory logic. They appear to reflect some independent standard of conduct that can override a promise, or at least have a limiting effect on its normative implications.

Clearly aware of the fact that the mitigation doctrine could not be explained as a plain implication of his understanding of contracts as promises, Fried describes it as 'a kind of altruistic duty . . . towards one's contractual partner, the more altruistic that it is directed to a partner in the wrong,' and justifies it further by noting that it is 'a duty without a cost, since the victim of the breach is never worse off for having mitigated,' and thus also 'a duty that recognizes that contractual liabilities are onerous enough that they should not be needlessly exacerbated.'[48] Now as we shall see, the fact that the 'duty' in question is costless (in the sense to which Fried allude) is indeed crucial in justifying its

---

[47] Understanding the mitigation requirement as something that arises out of friendship could possibly account for its special deontic status, for actions that are thought of as altruistic or supererogatory in other contexts are often rendered obligatory in the context of friendship and other forms of personal relations.

[48] Above n 12, at 131.

imposition. Yet it seems highly incongruous to argue that it is imposed *as an altruistic duty*. As Atiyah was quick to point out, '[c]onsidering the otherwise limited role of altruism in the liberal theory of contract, it does seem remarkable that one of its chief functions is to shield the promise-breaker from the full consequences of his wrong.'[49]

A more convincing explanation, and one that is far more harmonious with other aspects of the liberal approach to contract, can be found in the same set of considerations with which I explained earlier restrictions on remedial intervention more broadly. The key, again, is the harm principle. Here, too, the law can be explained as refraining from the imposition of a certain remedial duty where this could not be justified as the least demanding or restrictive way of preventing or redressing a given harm.

It could be pointed out in reply that there is a significant difference in this respect between cases governed by the mitigation rules and cases of the kind I discussed earlier. Whereas in the latter opting for a more moderate form of remedial intervention (eg from specific performance to expectation damages, from expectation to reliance damages, etc) can be straightforwardly justified by reference to the harm principle in light of the fact that the more moderate remedy simply suffices in order to redress (fully) or prevent the harm caused by the breach, in mitigation cases something still needs to be done—*and done by the innocent party*—in order for such a result to be achieved. This is true, and yet opting for a milder form of remedial intervention in both types of case can be understood as a step taken in the direction laid down by the harm principle, and close examination reveals that the step taken under the mitigation rules is in fact not that much bigger. Consider what exactly is left for the innocent party to do under the mitigation rules. This party is expected to act in its own interest (or to refrain from acting against its own interest), and more tellingly still, the mitigation doctrine, with its heavy reliance on standards of reasonableness, only applies in circumstances where acting in this manner involves very little in the way of effort, sacrifice, or compromise.[50] In such circumstances, the imposition on the defaulting party of a remedial duty that reflects the full value of contractual performance (or at any rate ignores the scope for reasonable mitigation, or allows for unreasonable exacerbation) would appear to be an unnecessary and excessive interference with this party's freedom despite the fact that it defaulted and despite the fact that the innocent party is, indeed, innocent.

---

[49] Above n 11, at 124. A proposal to base contractual relations more broadly on the morality of altruism was put forward by Duncan Kennedy in his well-known 'Form and Substance in Private Law Adjudication' (1976) 89 *Harvard Law Review* 1685. It is interesting to note that Fried himself forcefully rejects this analysis in the context of explaining the requirement of good faith. See above n 12, at 74–85.

[50] For a discussion and illustrations see Treitel, above n 31, at 910–15. For a comparative account see GH Treitel, *Remedies for Breach of Contract* (Oxford, 1988) 179–92. See also MG Bridge, 'Mitigation of Damages in Contract and the Meaning of Avoidable Loss' (1989) 105 *Law Quarterly Review* 398.

Thus contrary to Atiyah's contention, the mitigation rules, despite their potential effect (in the limited set of circumstances in which they apply) of stripping contractual obligations of some of their practical force, are not at odds with the notion that the core contractual obligation is performance.[51] It remains generally true that parties to contract are entitled to performance, and remains generally true that when in the aftermath of a breach performance is rendered impossible or undesirable, the innocent party is entitled to its full value. The mitigation rules are merely another illustration of the need to protect, and the possibility of protecting, contractual entitlements in line with the harm principle. Far from being at odds with the traditional liberal preference for performance remedies, the restraining effect of the mitigation rules is the liberal preference's natural concomitant. Indeed, far from being anathema to the liberal, these rules, inspired as they are—just like the more general principle to which they are an exception—by concern for personal freedom, can be understood as a direct consequence of the liberal approach.

The Freedom to Change One's Mind

A simple change of mind is but one of numerous eventualities that can lead to a breach of contract or to an intention to breach. Compared to other such eventualities ('frustration,' 'impossibility,' 'efficient breach' scenarios, etc) a change of mind is also the one that has probably received the least doctrinal and theoretical attention. Perhaps the reason for this is that the notion that a simple change of mind simply would not do is so intuitive and so well-enshrined. Indeed, traditional comparisons of contract to promise only serve to reinforce this intuition. If promises are sources of obligation, they provide promisors with exclusionary reasons to keep their promises. And if a simple change of mind is not amongst the excluded reasons, what is?

And yet, when Atiyah treats the freedom to change one's mind as a distinct value, and invokes it as such in his criticism of liberal theory of contract, his words do seem to me to strike a true chord. Focusing again on the traditional liberal preference for performance remedies, and with Fried's theory of contract in his sights, Atiyah wrote:

> Even the liberal theorist who rests on the moral obligatoriness of a promise may have twinges of anxiety over cases where the promisor has genuinely changed his mind and regrets the promise because he regrets the value judgment that led him to make it. Might there not be a case here for confining the damages to the promisee's reliance losses?[52]

[51] Above n 11, at 123–125.
[52] Above n 11, at 126.

He then went on to criticise Fried's rejection of change of mind as grounds for eluding contractual liability.[53] Now it may look as if the approach to remedies that I have advocated is even more restrictive than Fried's in this respect. While Fried rejects a change of mind as grounds for moving from expectation damages to reliance damages, his theory at least accommodates, as we have seen, the freedom to pay expectation damages rather than perform; whereas I argued in favour of specific performance as the standard remedy for breach, with the very move to expectation damages as requiring a justification, either as something that would not harm the innocent party, or by reference to the impracticality, the excessively harsh implications, or otherwise the undesirability of specific performance in a particular case or classes of cases.

The impression that the approach I have advocated is less amenable to a change of mind is, however, misleading. For although the value of the freedom to change one's mind has not been directly invoked, it is provided for to a considerable extent through the invocation of the harm principle as a principal restraint on remedial intervention in general, and as a possible ground for deviating from the standard response to a breach in particular.

The harm principle, as I have emphasised, is a principle of restraint reflecting concern for personal freedom. And the freedom to change one's mind is perhaps the paradigmatic form of personal freedom that the harm principle protects when it is brought to bear on the enforcement of contracts. As a value potentially holding justificatory power, the freedom to change one's mind has a special significance in cases that involve the voluntary assumption of obligations, for where no obligations are involved, a change of mind hardly ever requires a special justification; and where the obligations involved are not of the 'voluntarily assumed' kind, escaping them is not often a matter of changing one's mind. At the same time of all the various eventualities that can potentially lead to a breach of contract, a change of mind in particular is the one that touches on the issue of personal *freedom*—much more so than matters such as character flaw (eg when the breach is owed to dishonesty or opportunism on the part of the defaulting party), misfortune, or unpredictable changes in background circumstances.

The remedial regime I outlined above protects the freedom to change one's mind in a limited yet significant way. While protecting parties from the harmful effects of their counterparts' change of mind, it allows a change of mind whenever no such effects ensue and, subject to payment of damages (or the assumption of some other remedial duty), whenever the harm caused by a breach can be prevented or fully redressed by means other than (enforced) performance. This regime is more amenable to a change of mind than Fried's approach in that it provides that in cases where a deviation from the standard remedial response could be justified by reference to the harm principle, the breach requires no special excuse: the harm principle would, in such cases, do all the justificatory work

---

[53] For Fried's view see above n 12, at 17–21.

needed. (And remedial flexibility, and with it the freedom to change one's mind, is further enhanced by the provision that in assessing the harm caused to the innocent party, the focus is firmly on harm in terms of the denied benefits of a transaction and not on harm in terms of shattered relationships or personal insults; and in assessing the risk of institutional harm, the institution is understood as one that is meant to facilitate transactions, and not promote personal relations.)

And yet, in terms of the scope it allows for the freedom to change one's mind, the approach I have advocated does not escape Atiyah's charge altogether. The part it clearly does not escape is this:

> [S]ome people are much better at planning (their lives or their businesses) than others and therefore at making decisions which they are unlikely to want to change; other people are not very good at this, and constantly make decisions which they later regret. A moral or legal code which recognizes the prima facie binding force of an executory contract thus favours the first group at the expense of the second.[54]

Here Atiyah discusses what he calls 'the right to change one's mind' specifically in the context of calling into question the binding force (or the wisdom of acknowledging the binding force) of executory contracts, as distinguished from part-performed or partly relied-upon contracts. Now the remedial regime I have outlined allows for a change of mind, to the extent that it does, regardless of whether the contract at stake is (still) wholly executory or not. (Since the leading consideration in awarding remedies is to redress or prevent the harm caused to the innocent party in terms of denied contractual entitlements, whereas sometimes redressing this harm requires no more than awarding reliance damages even in a part-performed contract, in other cases it requires no less than specific performance even in executory contracts.) But Atiyah's charge would still apply even if the 'moral or legal code' in question only recognised the binding force of part-performed or partly relied-upon contracts: such a code would still 'favour' the first group of people he described. Of course nothing in what I said in this chapter is incompatible with the notion of the law taking measures to protect weak or vulnerable parties—vulnerable, that is, precisely in the sense of being likely to make decisions that they later regret—in special cases, or in special categories of contract or special categories of vulnerability (and more on this in the next chapter). Yet it remains true that in general, the practice is more accommodating to those who are good at planning their lives or their businesses than to those who 'constantly make decisions which they later regret.' I suspect, however, that this is inevitable. While the law can and should try to protect the latter from sheer exploitation by the former, and to some extent from their own incompetence, those with better foresight and better capacity to plan ahead are bound to fare better in a practice that is designed to facilitate the voluntary undertaking of obligations to others, with the inevitable restrictions on the free-

---

[54] Above n 45, at 168.

dom to change one's mind that go with that. Making the practice well and truly equally accommodating to both groups of people Atiyah described, by ruling out performance remedies altogether or by any other means, could only be achieved at the cost of subverting the practice's very essence and stripping it altogether of the values it is currently capable of promoting.

5

Freedom of Contract, Freedom from Contract

THE ASSOCIATION OF liberalism with the ideal of freedom of contract is quite natural. It is true that one does not have to subscribe to any moral, political or economic principle which is uniquely liberal in order to see freedom of contract as valuable. Yet as a political tradition—and as an approach to analysing contract law—liberalism has always provided particularly powerful arguments to the effect that people's ability voluntarily to undertake obligations to others is important, and hence that the legal practice of recognising and enforcing such obligations is of value, and is worthy of protection and promotion. The step from such a view to the endorsement of freedom of contract as a moral, political, and legal ideal is short and rather straightforward. Moreover (and for reasons which are less clear to me) the freedom of contract has sometimes been portrayed as a kind of flagship liberal doctrine, perhaps as the epitome of all the political freedoms liberalism stands for.[1]

However liberalism, as we began to see towards the end of the previous chapter, is not merely associated with the notion that people should enjoy the general ability and necessary institutional facilities to make contracts, or that they enjoy a considerable freedom to choose what kind of contracts to make and with whom to make them. The liberal approach to contract has often been associated with a particularly rigid conception of freedom of contract. It is a conception that entails an unrestricted, or very minimally restricted, freedom. It entails the freedom to make contracts and, when necessary, have them enforced (be it in the sense of actual enforcement, or in the sense of awarding performance damages), even in circumstances where various moral, economic or other considerations seem to justify, and sometimes cry out for, the imposition of some restrictions. It is a conception that, while perhaps compatible with demanding that the state provides the necessary frameworks within which to pursue contractual activity, allows the state a very limited role in shaping and regulating this activity.

---

[1] For a classic critique see GA Cohen, 'Capitalism, Freedom, and the Proletariat' in D Miller (ed), *Liberty* (Oxford, 1991).

It is not surprising that this rigid conception of freedom of contract has attracted stern criticism. The charge against it has been famously led by Patrick Atiyah. It has two facets: one descriptive, one normative. In his seminal *The Rise and Fall of Freedom of Contract*,[2] Atiyah documented the rise to prominence of freedom of contract as a political, economic, and legal ideal, the high point of which he put around 1870; and from then on, for about a hundred years, the gradual decline of the ideal—a process by which '[f]reedom of choice was whittled down in many directions, government regulation replaced free contract, . . . and paternalism once again was the order of the day.'[3] Indeed, modern law (and here I follow Atiyah in focusing on English law, but similar trends can be identified in legal systems throughout the industrialised world) interferes with and restricts the freedom of contract in numerous areas and by numerous means. Identifiable grounds for intervention with this freedom are sometimes egalitarian in nature, sometimes redistributive, sometimes paternalistic (or any combination thereof).[4] The law takes measures to protect various types of relatively weak or vulnerable contract parties—consumers,[5] employees,[6] tenants[7]—sometimes in general, sometimes in specific categories of contract or commercial activity.[8] Intervention is introduced in some cases in the name of protecting contracting individuals, in others in the name of public (economic or other) interests.[9] The law sometimes dictates contractual terms,[10] introduces special requirements for the formation of certain contracts,[11] or prohibits or imposes sanctions for a refusal to contract with certain parties or in certain circumstances;[12] it sometimes renders agreed terms illegal,[13] void,[14] voidable,[15] or unenforceable,[16] and sometimes limits the obtainable remedy for breach. And apart from various forms of statutory intervention, courts have

[2] Oxford, 1979.

[3] PS Atiyah, *Essays on Contract* (Oxford,1986), Essay 12: 'Freedom of Contract and the New Right', at 356.

[4] For Atiyah's overview see above n 3, Essay 6: 'The Liberal Theory of Contract'. The precise nature (paternalistic, redistributive, etc) of particular forms of intervention in the freedom of contract is of course a matter of much debate which need not be addressed here.

[5] See eg Unfair Contract Terms Act 1977.

[6] See eg Employment Protection (Consolidation) Act 1978; Employment Act 1989; Trade Union and Labour Relations (Consolidation) Act 1992, s 137(1)(a).

[7] See eg Rent Act 1977; Landlord and Tenant Act 1985.

[8] See eg Consumer Credit Act 1974; Financial Services Act 1986.

[9] See eg Fair Trading Act 1973; Restrictive Trade Practices Act 1977; Competition Act 1980. (For an overview see M Griffiths, *Law for Purchasing and Supply* (2nd edn, 1996) 263–72.)

[10] See eg Sex Discrimination Act 1975, s 8; Unfair Contract Terms Act 1977, s 6; Landlord and Tenant Act 1985, s 8.

[11] See eg Consumer Credit Act 1974, ss 55(1), 61, 62, 63, 64(5) (various requirements of form); Insurance Companies Act 1982, s 76; Timeshare Act 1992, ss 2–4 ('cooling off' period).

[12] See eg Resale Prices Act 1976, ss 12, 25; Race Relations Act 1976, Pts II, III and ss 56, 57, 62.

[13] See generally GH Treitel, *The Law of Contract* (10th edn, London, 1999) ch 11.

[14] See eg Insurance Companies Act 1982, s 36; Pension Schemes Act 1993, s 160(1)(a); Race Relations Act 1977, s 72(1)–(2).

[15] See Treitel, above n 13, at 505–8.

[16] See eg Consumer Credit Act 1974, s 40(1); Financial Services Act 1986, ss 5, 6, 56, 57, 131, 132.

routinely applied broad interpretations of various contract law doctrines—fraud, duress, implied terms, consideration, unconscionability—to impose further conditions for the validity or enforceability of contracts, and to protect parties further from the consequences of unfortunate, yet genuine, exercises of their very freedom to make contracts.[17] And while in *The Rise and Fall of Freedom of Contract* Atiyah described the decline of the ideal during the hundred years or so since 1870, and even speculated that by the end of this period the pendulum had swung to its furthest point away from the ideal, there appear to be no conclusive signs of a considerable swing in the other direction. If anything, in Europe at least, EC policy indicates that the trend towards further protection, further regulation, further inroads into the freedom of contract is, early in the twenty-first century, in rude health.[18]

Thus on the descriptive level, it can easily be concluded that the rigid conception of freedom in contract is highly unrealistic. Even more damaging, however, is the normative facet of the charge against this conception. Without going into any detail, suffice it to say that many, probably most, of the instances of intervention in freedom of contract that are to be found in modern legal systems appear to be justified. They often fit neatly into desirable social, economic, and legal policies, and reflect perfectly valid (and sometimes overlapping) concerns—for vulnerable individuals, for social justice, for individual and public well-being. Moreover, the goals and considerations that many forms of intervention in freedom of contract reflect are of the kind that liberals in particular (with the possible exception of hard-core libertarians) usually find hard to resist. It is against this background that the sentiment (if not quite the literal meaning) of Atiyah's inference that '[w]hatever its normative power as a matter of philosophical or political argument . . . liberal theory seems unlikely to carry the day in a democratic society,'[19] may ring true.

My aim in this chapter is not to defend a rigid conception of freedom of contract. Rather, it is to cast doubt on the very notion that liberalism in general, or the liberal approach to contract law in particular, entails anything like it. The debate itself, as many readers will recognise, is by no means new. Over a hundred years ago, and in connection with the tellingly nicknamed 'liberal legislation' of the late nineteenth century, TH Green sought to disprove views similar to those with which I wish to take issue here, and his arguments were similar in orientation to much of what I shall argue in what follows.[20] Yet the modern theoretical challenge to the liberal approach, paradigmatically exemplified in Atiyah's work, is somewhat more sophisticated than that faced by Green in his

[17] See Atiyah, above n 4, at 127–33 and references there.

[18] See eg the Directive on Unfair Terms in Consumer Contracts (Council Directive 93/13/EEC, OJL 95, 21.4.1993, p 29). For a discussion see H Beale, 'Legislative Control of Fairness: The Directive on Unfair Terms in Consumer Contracts' in J Beatson and D Friedmann (eds), *Good Faith and Fault in Contract Law* (Oxford, 1995) 231. For an overview see 'Introduction' by the editors, at 3.

[19] Above n 4, at 128.

[20] See 'Liberal Legislation and Freedom of Contract' in TH Green, *Lectures on the Principles of Political Obligation and Other Writing* (P Harris and J Morrow (eds), Cambridge, 1986), 194.

time. And this, combined with the ever accelerating trend towards further inroads into freedom of contract, warrants re-examination of the relationship between liberalism and the scope of this freedom.

The popularity of the notion that the liberal approach entails an extreme conception of freedom of contract is owed in small part to a certain misconception of the nature of contract or contract law, and in large part to some misunderstandings concerning liberalism itself. Regarding contract, the misconception in question is related to the common failure to recognise the pertinent dissimilarities between contract and promise—the very dissimilarities I aimed to expose in earlier chapters. Although this failure need not be unique to proponents of liberal theory, the liberal frame of reference, as Charles Fried's work illustrates vividly, has always been a comfortable habitat for the 'contract as promise' approach, and is often identified with it. Yet considerations related to the differences between contract and promise will this time play a fairly modest role in the discussion to follow. They will, I hope, lend further support to conclusions arrived at regardless. The main problems in this area, however, lie elsewhere.

As for liberalism, the main error in question is its understanding as, necessarily, a doctrine of limited government. Another, sometimes related, error is the understanding of liberalism as committed to moral individualism.[21] The finest modern interpretation of liberalism as neither is Joseph Raz's. The version of liberalism that Raz defends regards government as a possible source of freedom, and not just a potential threat to it. It leaves considerable scope for 'perfectionist' action by the state, and it allows for perfectionist action to be taken in pursuit of non-individualistic goals.[22] But here I will not set out to defend, at least not directly, this or any other particular version of liberal theory. Instead I wish to comment on two more local themes that tend to surface in discussions of the liberal approach to the freedom of contract, and on which the association of liberalism with a particularly rigid conception of this ideal typically hinges. The first theme is neutrality; the second and more significant theme is personal autonomy. My aim in so doing is twofold. This way, I hope to provide the liberal approach to contract law with a broader, more robust defence, for I will aim to cast doubt on the notion that liberalism more generally, and not just in Razian form, entails a particularly rigid conception of freedom of contract. The analysis of these two themes, however, should eventually provide some indirect support for that version of liberalism to which I subscribe, and bring it to the fore as the broader inspiration for many of my arguments.

[21] The two are sometimes related because individualism excludes the promotion of a certain range of values and goals from being considered as valid grounds for government action. As such it is a source, although by no means the only source, of 'limited government' arguments.

[22] See generally *The Morality of Freedom* (Oxford, 1986).

Neutrality

Neutrality is but one of several principles of governmental restraint. As least since John Rawls' influential advocacy of a doctrine of neutral political concern, however, it has become fairly dominant in contemporary liberal thought, and a principle with which liberalism is often identified.[23] Thus in his criticism of the liberal theory of contract, Atiyah attributes to the 'true liberal' the view according to which 'contract law is "neutral," once given the capacities and individual abilities of contracting parties . . . and once given the existing distribution of wealth and entitlements.'[24] As a principle of political action, neutrality embraces two closely related ideas: neutrality between conceptions of the good, and neutrality between individuals.[25] Adherence to the principle of neutrality essentially entails striving to help or hinder the parties concerned in an equal degree.[26] And the basic idea behind the invocation of neutrality in the context of examining the liberal attitude to the freedom of contract is that most forms of intervention in the freedom of contract represent a deviation from a policy of neutral concern. When the law protects the relatively vulnerable party against the strong, for instance, it is not neutral between contracting parties: it helps the former and hinders the latter; or when the law strikes down contracts or contract terms on grounds of immorality, it is not neutral between competing conceptions of the good: it hinders the pursuit of some such conceptions, and in the process promotes or encourages the pursuit of alternative ones.

It is along these lines that Atiyah, having attributed to the true liberal a commitment to the neutrality of contract law, argues that this commitment prevents the liberal from recognising the redistributive nature of legal doctrines through the use of which freedom of contract is overridden, let alone from *endorsing* doctrines that clearly have a redistributive effect.[27] Now the most profound reply would be to point out that in fact, not all liberals are committed to the principle of neutrality. Indeed, that version of liberalism to which I expressed

---

[23] See eg discussion by Michael Freeden in *Ideologies and Political Theory: A Conceptual Approach* (Oxford, 1997) 259–75. See also J Rawls, *Political Liberalism* (New York, 1993) 190–95. For Rawls' classic account see *A Theory of Justice* (Cambridge, Massachusetts, 1971).

[24] Above n 4, at 133.

[25] See Raz, above n 22, at 111–12.

[26] See A Montefiore in Montefiore (ed), *Neutrality and Impartiality* (Cambridge, 1975) 5; and see Raz's distinction between principled neutrality and by-product neutrality, above n 22, at 113. Some writers understand neutrality as a principle according to which ideals of the good should be excluded as grounds for political action, or at least fail to distinguish between exclusion of ideals and neutrality between ideals. As I believe the latter to be the correct explanation of political neutrality, the former doctrine and its implications for freedom of contract will not be addressed directly here. As both doctrines are often inspired by concern for personal autonomy, however, the subsequent discussion of autonomy is relevant to both.

[27] Above n 4, at 132ff. The example around which Atiyah builds this argument is that of the doctrine of unconscionability, but the argument applies equally to other cases that involve, as he put it, 'overriding the result of a deal or bargain voluntarily agreed by sane adults' in order to protect the more vulnerable party.

my allegiance earlier eschews this principle, along with its wholesale rejection of anti-perfectionism.[28] Nevertheless, I wish to indicate my main reasons for thinking that the conceptual link between neutrality and an uncompromising conception of freedom of contract is not as straightforward or obvious as it may appear to be.

Neutrality, Fairness and Inequality of Bargaining Power

Neutrality is characteristically defended as a means to a fair contest. Yet even if or inasmuch as it is thought that neutrality is generally desirable, or that acting neutrally is sometimes or often the fairest way to act, there are bound to be cases where it is clearly neither. A primary type of case where neutrality might not be fair is that which involves a contest wherein there is a severe power imbalance between the competing parties. Of course not all contests that involve a power imbalance require non-neutral treatment (referees are justly expected to be neutral when Manchester United plays Oxford United). But some clearly do. Montefiore's example of a dispute between two children, where a decision by their father to remain neutral would amount to a decision to allow the physically stronger child to prevail, is one such case.[29] Whether or not a given power-imbalance renders neutral treatment unfair would depend on the interplay of considerations such as the nature and magnitude of the imbalance, its source and legitimacy, the way in which it is used in a given contest, and of course the nature of the contest and the type of treatment at stake.[30] But it can be stated with some certainty that at least in some of the cases where the law overrides the freedom of contract, the gap in resources (economic and otherwise) and bargaining power between the parties in question is such that a general policy of helping or hindering both in an equal degree would not even have the appearance of fairness. Familiar legal restrictions on landlords in their dealings with tenants or on employers in their dealings with employees, or the striking down of certain kinds of product liability disclaimers and monopolistic arrangements, can hardly be objected to on grounds of fairness or by reference to the intuitive appeal of neutrality as a means to a fair contest.

Here it could be pointed out that the argument thus far, rather than indicating that neutrality does not entail a rigid conception of freedom of contract, sug-

---

[28] See Raz, above n 22, especially chs 5, 6.

[29] Above n 26, at 7. See also Raz's discussion of this example, above n 22, at 114.

[30] For an illustration of the complexities involved, consider again the Manchester United–Oxford United example. A gap in footballing prowess between competing clubs is a simple example of an imbalance that does not justify a non-neutral treatment *by the referee*. Yet the same kind of imbalance (ie between competing clubs or teams, and (ignoring for the moment the additional possibility of an economic imbalance, which clearly features in the original example) purely in terms of sporting prowess) could justify a deviation from a neutral policy when agencies other than the referee are concerned. A good example for a non-neutral policy in such a context comes from the American National Basketball Association. The player recruitment procedure adopted by the NBA (known as 'the draft') assigns weaker teams priority over stronger ones in selecting new players.

gests that neutrality cannot be defended so easily as a principle of political action in the first place. After all, endorsing neutrality as a principle of political action involves assigning it lexical priority over (at least certain) other principles of action, and not merely seeing it as sometimes desirable and sometimes not. This being the case, the argument thus far at least demonstrates that the fairness-minded liberal would consider the rigid conception of the freedom of contract, or at any rate some of the implications of this conception, as a possible reason to reject or at least modify the principle of neutrality rather than as an illustration of the principle's general suitability.

A case in point is Robert Nozick's reasoning in *Anarchy, State, and Utopia*.[31] For someone who seems to take it almost for granted that a legitimate government must be neutral—'*unscrupulously*' so—between its citizens, it is perhaps surprising to see how willingly he concedes that in certain contexts the state is allowed, or indeed required, to act in a seemingly non-neutral way.[32] This is so, he contends, so long as the state's action can be justified *independently*, that is as something which is designed to achieve some goal other than the differential treatment of citizens for its own sake. Thus in its capacity as an enforcer of contracts, one capacity which Nozick alludes to specifically in his succinct discussion of the (seemingly) non-neutral state, non-neutral action can presumably be justified as a means of protecting one party from, say, being exploited by the other. But then according to Nozick, in such cases the state in fact remains neutral:

> That a prohibition thus independently justifiable works out to affect different persons differently is no reason to condemn is as nonneutral, provided it was instituted or continues for (something like) the reasons which justify it, and not in order to yield differential benefits.[33]

Now, if so, then neutrality does not entail, not even prima facie, a particularly stringent restriction of the state's right (or duty? privilege?) to interfere with freedom of contract. However, it has been argued, and to my mind correctly, that in light of that open-ended allowance made for 'independent' justification, Nozick's principle of government action cannot be described as a true principle of neutrality, and the state that adheres to it is not a neutral state.[34]

The Possibility of Neutrality

Even inasmuch as it is thought that the principle of neutrality is acceptable, adherence to it is not always possible. At least in circumstances where it is impossible either to help all the parties concerned or to hinder all the parties concerned (and help or hinder in an equal degree), the possibility of neutrality depends on the practicality in the circumstances of the distinction between not

---

[31] New York, 1974.
[32] *Ibid* at 33, 272–73.
[33] *Ibid* at 273.
[34] See Raz, above n 22, at 114–16.

helping and hindering (or similarly the distinction between not hindering and helping). This is so because in such circumstances one can only remain neutral by not helping nor hindering *any* of the parties, whereas if by not helping a party one also hinders it (or, similarly, if by not hindering a party one also helps it), then one could only be neutral if one could help, or hinder, both parties (and in an equal degree).[35]

It is impossible to help both parties or hinder both parties in situations where intervention can only be in the form of taking sides in the contest.[36] Many of the cases where the law affects contractual activity clearly fall into this category. In deciding whether or not to allow a contract term which would greatly benefit banks but which would spell disaster for many a loan taker, for instance, the options are to help the latter (and, by this, hinder the former) or vice versa; and whether or not it is thought possible to help neither, no single decision would help both or hinder both at the same time. As for the practicality of the distinction between not helping and hindering, this problem comes into sharp relief in the context of the state's responsibility to its citizens in general. Inasmuch as it is thought that it is the state's duty to help its citizens, its failure to help amounts to hindering. The exact scope of the state's responsibility to its citizens is of course a matter of much debate, and it is in fact this very debate which underlies much of the discussion concerning the acceptability of various principles of neutrality (and other anti-perfectionist principles). Yet regardless of one's view concerning the precise scope of the state's responsibility to its citizens in general, it remains true that the state's inevitable involvement in and effect on contractual activity are such that in many cases it is bound to help certain parties and hinder others, or at any rate help certain parties and not help others, with the option of not helping nor hindering non-existent.[37]

[35] In his discussion of the significance of the distinction between not helping and hindering for the possibility of neutrality (*ibid* at 120–21), Raz at one point can be understood as implying that neutrality is never possible in cases where the distinction cannot be drawn. Yet the example he gives in this context does not prove this. The example involves two warring countries, a commodity which is in short supply in one country but not in the other, and a third country arguably in a position where, on the assumption that not helping amounts to hindering, it would have to start providing the country which is in short supply with the commodity in question in order to remain neutral—something which is clearly incompatible with the common understanding of neutrality. However the example is not of a case where neutrality is impossible. For even if it is true that by not providing the first country with the commodity in question the third country hinders it, and hinders it more than it does the second country in this respect, by providing the first country the third country would nevertheless be breaking its neutrality, since it would be helping one side but not the other (helping is still helping even if not helping is hindering). The third country could, however, remain neutral by offsetting its help to the first country by helping the second, by whatever means, in an equal degree. This demonstrates that it is only in cases where either helping or hindering both parties is impossible that the possibility of neutrality depends on that of drawing the distinction between not helping and hindering.

[36] There are other types of situation where helping both parties or hindering both parties would be impossible, eg in cases where it is simply impossible to have any effect on the predicament of one (or more) of the parties concerned.

[37] By the state's *involvement* in contractual activity here I do not refer to its possible involvement as a party to contracts, but rather to its role in creating the normative and institutional framework for contractual activity, enforcing contracts, etc.

The reason for this is simple. Contractual activity is pursued within a framework which is largely created, and the boundaries of which are largely defined, by the state. Moreover, this framework incorporates the state's adjudicating and enforcing agencies. Thus, for instance, by defining the framework in a way which enables a certain 'strong' party to capitalise on the vulnerability of a certain 'weak' party, the state—the law—does not merely fail to help the latter: it plays an active role in creating the conditions for its fall. Similarly, by acknowledging the validity of such contracts and, when necessary, making its adjudicating and enforcing mechanisms available to the former, the state does not merely fail to hinder the strong party, but actively helps it: first by creating a framework in which it prevails, and then in securing the rewards.

This argument does not show that in all cases of intervention in the freedom of contract neutrality is impossible. But it shows that this is often the case, namely whenever the matter at stake falls under both categories: it is impossible to help or hinder both parties, and impossible, in practical terms, to draw the distinction between not helping and hindering. Now, could it be argued in reply that in such cases the state can still maintain its neutrality, or best approximate neutrality, as long as it defines the boundaries of contractual activity in as broad terms as possible, with as little intervention as possible in the freedom of contract? Or that the state can remain neutral as long as it does not do anything *in order* to help or hinder any particular party, but generally strives to do as little as possible, leaving it to the parties themselves to settle their affairs? By the same token it could probably be argued that even in enforcing contracts the state can remain wholly (or sufficiently) neutral, as long as all it does is give effect to what the parties did, rather than to any non-neutral standards which were imposed on them. But to argue along such lines is to be guilty of a confusion between non-action (or minimal action) and neutral action. To be neutral one has to strive to help or hinder all the parties concerned in an equal degree. If one's action is not designed to achieve this, and in practice one helps one party more than the other (or helps one party and hinders the other, or helps one party and not the other, etc), then one is not neutral, whether one's effect on the parties' standing was the result of action or non-action. Perhaps a policy of minimal action or minimal intervention in the freedom of contract could still be advocated in cases where neutrality is impossible; in such cases, however, it could be advocated as an anti-perfectionist policy, but not specifically as a policy of neutral concern.

At this juncture it would be appropriate to turn to the other theme I mentioned earlier, that of personal autonomy. I said that autonomy is a more significant theme in the present discussion than neutrality. One reason for this is that neutrality, as well as other anti-perfectionist principles, is often justified on grounds of concern for personal autonomy.[38] Another reason is that whereas, as I said at the outset, neutrality is not an essential feature of liberalism—certainly

---

[38] See eg J Rawls, *A Theory of Justice* (Cambridge, Massachusetts, 1971) 252ff; and see Raz, above n 22, at 108, 130–33.

not of that version of liberalism to which I subscribe—commitment to the protection and promotion of personal autonomy certainly is. This last claim should be qualified: the deeper concern that underlies that for autonomy (at least as far as this version of liberalism is concerned) is for people's prospects of having good lives; and as for principles of government, the deeper commitment of this version of liberalism (though not only this version, and not only liberalism) is to the notion that governments should do their best to help people have good lives. And in certain socio-historical contexts personal autonomy is wholly irrelevant in this respect, while in others it may be of no more than marginal significance. However in the context of the modern industrialised world, a good life *means*, to a great, and probably growing, extent, a good *autonomous* life.[39] The alleged connection between personal autonomy and freedom of contract thus goes to the heart of the matter before us.

Personal Autonomy

Personal autonomy is an ideal of self-creation, of people exerting control over their destinies. An autonomous life consists in the pursuit of freely chosen activities, goals and relationships.[40] The basic assumption in invoking the value of personal autonomy in discussions of the liberal conception of freedom of contract is similar to that behind its common invocation in discussions concerning the binding force of promises. Generally speaking, acknowledgement of the value of personal autonomy entails concern for the conditions which are necessary in order for people to lead autonomous lives, as well as (prima facie) respect for people's freely chosen pursuits. The assumption is that to allow people voluntarily to undertake obligations and to acknowledge the binding force of such obligations (and, as far as contracts are concerned, when necessary to enforce them) is to show respect for people's autonomy; whereas to prevent people from voluntarily undertaking obligations or to fail to acknowledge the binding force of such obligations is to show disrespect for their autonomy.[41]

I do not wish to deny the basic truth of this assumption. In fact I agree that it provides a valid starting point for discussions of the binding force of promises and contracts, and similarly a valid starting point from which to appreciate the moral significance of freedom of contract, and I will use it as such. The point I wish to illustrate, however, is that it is no more than a basic, and as such a rather crude, assumption—indeed no more than a starting point; and that as such it can easily be (and has been) misinterpreted, and its implications in terms of the appropriate scope for the freedom of contract can easily be exaggerated or mis-

---

[39] See Raz, 'Liberty and Trust' in RP George (ed), *Natural Law, Liberalism, and Morality* (Oxford, 1996) 113, and above n 22, at 369–70.

[40] See *ibid*.

[41] See, eg C Fried, *Contract as Promise: A Theory of Contractual Obligation* (Cambridge, Massachusetts, 1981) 20–21; Atiyah, above n 4, at 145.

understood. The interrelated and partly overlapping considerations that I shall now introduce, in what I consider an increasing order of significance, are meant to establish just that.

Preliminaries

My first preliminary point is the simple reminder that while the recognition of the value of personal autonomy is prominent in modern liberal theory, it is by no means the only value that liberal theory accommodates, nor the only legitimate inspiration for political action it may endorse. Even a government which is highly committed to promoting autonomy may recognise cases where the promotion of other values or goals, or the prevention of some undesirable occurrences, justifies a course of action that does not promote autonomy as much as some alternative course of action would, or does not promote it at all, or even has the side effect of restricting it.[42] In such cases, it is possible that the reasons for embarking on that course of action simply outweigh conflicting reasons which derive from the value of personal autonomy. This is true even with regard to individualistic liberalism, and is doubly significant given the possibility, and merit, of non-individualistic liberalism, which accommodates and advocates the promotion of various values and goals over and above the individualistic ones, let alone over and above respect for individual free choice as such. Thus the very desirability of certain non-autonomy-enhancing (or even autonomy-restricting) policies does not in itself indicate that liberal theory is morally flawed, just as the very existence or the wide acceptance of certain non-autonomy-enhancing policies does not in itself prove that liberal theory is out of touch with reality.

Like the rest of the considerations I will introduce in this section, the second preliminary point aims to show that regardless of the possibility of autonomy-derived reasons being outweighed, the notion that concern for personal autonomy entails respect for freedom of contract (or, for that matter, freedom of promise) does not itself entail and need not presuppose the proposition that respect is due to *every* promissory or contractual undertaking, nor indeed the proposition that the binding force of every promissory undertaking, wholly regardless of its content and implications, must be acknowledged due to it being an expression of the free will of a sane adult.

Perhaps the most elementary objection to this fallacy has to do with morally repugnant undertakings. Moral individualism in particular is sometimes understood as committed to the view that since the binding force of voluntary undertakings in general derives from the value of personal autonomy, then the

---

[42] It could be argued that at least from the perspective of humanistic political morality, every course of governmental action, be it in protecting wildlife, banning the use of recreational drugs, or beautifying the capital city, must ultimately be justifiable as doing something good *for people*. Yet the point remains the same: as these three examples illustrate, not everything that is good for people is good because it enhances autonomy.

binding force, prima facie at least, of even a morally repugnant promise must be acknowledged. Although that version of liberalism which underlies the current discussion is not grounded in such morality, it is again worth noting that not even individualists need be guilty of such a fundamental error. Even from an individualistic perspective, that is, it should be possible to identify cases where the undesirability of certain voluntary undertakings, even by sane adults, pre-cludes them from acquiring binding force or warranting any kind of respect. (Most philosophical individualists, for instance, would deny the notion that by promising to commit a rape a person can, as long as he or she is a sane adult, assume a prima facie obligation to rape.) Since my aim here is not to defend moral individualism, I will not try to account for the precise nature of the argu-ments with which the individualist may support such a conclusion. To put the matter in general terms, an attempt at undertaking an obligation can only be successful as long as it falls within the spectrum of obligations that it is judged to be morally desirable or at any rate *permissible* for people to have or be able to assume. The real difference between individualistic and non-individualistic morality in this respect is simply that the latter draws on a much richer variety of normative sources in defining this spectrum. And in the framework of non-individualistic liberal theory it is particularly plain to see that commitment to the value of personal autonomy notwithstanding, the normative consequences of an attempt at a voluntary undertaking of an obligation are not entirely deter-mined by the free will of the individual. The liberal commitment to the protec-tion and promotion of personal autonomy does not even entail that every promise is prima facie binding, and, with this in mind, I will now try to show in slightly greater detail how the liberal's principled refusal to acknowledge the binding force of particular promises, like her willingness to endorse certain poli-cies and decisions that amount to overriding freedom of contract, may extend to matters beyond morally repugnant undertakings.

Autonomy-Derived Value as a Matter of Degree

A somewhat more subtle fallacy is the notion that all the promises or all the con-tracts or contract terms that are not judged to fall outside of that 'spectrum of permissibility' I described in the previous paragraph are equally meaningful, sig-nificant, or valuable exercises of personal autonomy. Rather, some are clearly more meaningful than others, and some are hardly meaningful or not at all.

The kind of exaggeration and ultimately confusion that can result from overlooking the fact that a (legitimate) promise's value as an expression of per-sonal autonomy may well be a matter of degree are illustrated vividly in Atiyah's analysis of the famous 'Reading Pipes' case,[43] in which a dispute arose (in part) over a builder's substitution of the contractually specified pipes with

---

[43] *Jacob & Youngs v Kent*, 129 NE 889 (1921).

pipes of a similar design and quality but of a different make. In his analysis of the case, Atiyah argued that for the court to force the buyer to pay for the house despite the fact that it had been fitted with a different make of pipes, would be 'to show disrespect for the buyer's autonomy, his free choice'; and that the apparent unreasonableness of the alternative decision (ie to allow the buyer to escape payment) is 'surely because we no longer have quite the same respect for individual autonomy and free choice.'[44] But the gravity of such a display of disrespect for autonomy can only be discerned in proportion to the significance which can be attached to that particular expression of autonomy or free choice to which disrespect was allegedly shown, and in proportion to the weight of the reasons for so doing (that is, for showing such disrespect). The question that should be asked in analysing such a case from the perspective of personal autonomy is just how significant an expression of autonomy is a person's wish to have his house equipped with 'Reading' pipes rather than with virtually identical pipes of a different make. The rather obvious answer to this (in the circumstances of the case, at any rate), in conjunction with the fact that the decision to make the buyer pay was supported by weighty considerations that can themselves be accommodated by liberal theory, shows that although the decision indeed seems perfectly justified, this case and similar cases fall some way short of exposing the liberal concern for personal autonomy, or liberalism in general, as an inadequate basis on which to explain modern contract law.

Respect for Autonomy as Ground for Restricting Freedom

The next consideration is broader and farther-reaching. Respect for personal autonomy itself, to the extent that it has a significant bearing on the desirable scope and the normative implications of contractual activity, does not always entail more rather than less freedom, or less rather than more intervention in freedom of contract. The matter that calls for attention here is the relationship between personal autonomy and the availability of options. As the ideal of personal autonomy is intrinsically related to free choice, having a sufficient range of options to choose from is (among other things) an indispensable condition of autonomy.[45] Yet the notion that, in practical terms, respect for autonomy simply translates to a policy of creating, or at least leaving open, *as many* options as possible for those whose autonomy is at stake to choose from, is a grave misconception, and one which is responsible for much of the misunderstanding concerning the liberal approach to freedom of contract.

Certain options can have the effect of reducing one's overall autonomy, or one's chances of leading an autonomous life, even if chosen freely. Discouraging

---

[44] Above n 4, at 145.
[45] See Raz, above n 22, at 204, 372–77.

or even preventing a person from choosing such an option can quite straight-forwardly be justified as a means of protecting her autonomy, of preventing her from compromising it through one rash or ill-calculated, albeit free, decision. Examples of such options abound, and the logic of eliminating them as a means of protecting, rather than undermining, autonomy is apparent in many instances of intervention in the freedom of contract. To take one, a decision to enter an employment contract that imposes far-reaching restrictions on alternative employment in future can clearly have an adverse long-term effect on a person's autonomy. Far from incompatible with respect for personal autonomy, eliminating the risk of people being tempted into such contracts seems to be required by it.

The predictable response to this line of argument is the proposition that personal autonomy would be better enhanced if rather than eliminating options that, if chosen, may undermine autonomy or be otherwise disadvantageous, such options were left open so that people could avoid them independently, as something that is itself an exercise of personal autonomy. A general argument to a similar effect—one that recommends the unlimited availability of bad options as something which is invariably conducive to autonomy or free will—has been thoroughly rebutted by Raz.[46] In a nutshell, his point was that the elimination of certain bad options (let us say, the *really* bad ones) brings us nowhere near a situation where there are no bad options at all for people to avoid autonomously: plenty of bad options, and opportunities freely to choose not to pursue them, are bound to remain. Yet over and above this, in the context of the freedom of contract the argument at stake can be shown to be particularly ill-fated. Again, the point has to do with inequality of bargaining power. Given the kind of inequality between parties that most known forms of intervention in the freedom of the contract seek to address, a general policy of leaving it to the parties to discern the bad options and 'freely' avoid them would often amount to endorsing a state of affairs whereby many have nothing but bad options to choose from. Indeed, such a state of affairs was precisely what much of the so-called liberal legislation that TH Green strove to justify in the nineteenth century sought to redress.[47]

The last paragraph focused on the possibility of options which, if chosen, would tend to undermine the autonomy of those who choose them. A close possibility—if you want, the other side of the same coin—is that of options which, if chosen, would have the effect of undermining the autonomy not of those who choose them but of others. The point that was made earlier applies here just the same: the elimination of such options can as straightforwardly be justified as a means of protecting autonomy. A law that deprives employers of the option of offering exploitative, unfair, or highly restrictive employment

---

[46] See above n 22, at 380–81.
[47] See above n 20.

contracts need not be justified differently from a law that deprives prospective employees of the option of accepting such offers. If anything, inasmuch as it is thought that the more clearly paternalistic (or paternalistically-formulated, or paternalistically-motivated) laws require a special justificatory component over and above what is required to justify their non-paternalistic equivalents, then laws of the latter kind are easier to justify. Indeed, none of my arguments thus far is in any way incompatible with the (plausible) notion that people should generally enjoy greater freedom to compromise their own autonomy than to undermine others'. The point is merely that forms of restriction of freedom of contract that are aimed at preventing either could be justified as a means of protecting autonomy.

To reiterate, the argument thus far is all that is needed in order to reject the suggested incompatibility of the liberal commitment to the value of personal autonomy with many instances of intervention in the freedom of contract. Atiyah was surely correct when he wrote that:

> [the argument that] to prevent a person, even in his own interests, from binding himself is to show disrespect for his moral autonomy, can ring very hollow when used to defend a grossly unfair contract secured at the expense of a person of little understanding or bargaining skill.[48]

But grossly unfair contracts are often considered grossly unfair precisely because they have an adverse long-term effect on the autonomy of the persons 'at the expense of' which they were secured. Clearly in such cases respect for personal autonomy, rather than be used in defence of the contract, can be invoked as a reason to disallow it or to limit some of its legal implications.

The Value of Autonomy and the Pursuit of the Good

Perhaps the broadest and most fundamental consideration has yet to be introduced. The specific effect of undermining autonomy (of those who choose them or of others) need not be the only criterion for identifying options which respect for personal autonomy does not require us to allow, or even requires us to eliminate. The broader point, again one which was famously defended by Raz, is that personal autonomy is valuable only when exercised in pursuit of the good.[49] An autonomous life is valuable when spent in the (at least to some extent successful) pursuit of valuable activities and relationships, but not otherwise. The pursuit of racist activities or, for instance, or the pursuit of exploitative relationships, is in fact much worse, morally speaking, when done autonomously, by a person who makes a free and well-informed decision to

---

[48] Above n 4, at 148.
[49] See Raz, above n 22, at 378–81.

engage in it, than when done for lack of choice, for instance, or out of sheer ignorance.[50]

The fact that personal autonomy is generally dependent for its value on the worthiness of its exercise is indeed the wider basis on which to arrive at the conclusions that have already emerged in the discussion thus far. To lead valuable, autonomous lives, people need a sufficient range of valuable options to choose from, but they do not need worthless options, let alone *all* the worthless options; and while promoting personal autonomy requires, among other things, making available a sufficient range of valuable options, it does not entail a favourable attitude to the availability of bad ones. On the contrary: when the availability of certain bad options would significantly decrease people's chances of leading valuable autonomous lives, or exercising their autonomy in a valuable way in particular circumstances, or more generally leading valuable lives, concern for autonomy could only require their elimination.

It is still possible to argue that in certain situations and under certain conditions, the availability of certain bad options could be conducive to personal autonomy, namely when and inasmuch as the wrong choice could serve as an experience through which the agent's propensity or competence to choose correctly in future would be enhanced. This may indeed sound plausible in the context of contractual activity: people can learn from their mistakes, and the odd bad bargain may, in the long term, help to hone a person's competence to strike better deals. It is important to note that the combined effect of the arguments thus far was not to deny this possibility, nor to support a policy of restricting contractual freedom to an extent that would make its realisation impossible. My aim is not to defend a policy designed to ensure that all legally valid or legally enforceable transactions are genuine, mutually-advantageous bargains, or that they are the best bargains that the parties could possibly strike. Rather, it is to cast doubt on the alleged connection between the liberal approach and the other extreme: an extreme conception of the *freedom* of contract—and

---

[50] See *ibid* at 380. Raz's argument (on which I rely here) to the effect that personal autonomy is only valuable when exercised in pursuit of the good was criticised, to my mind unsuccessfully, by Jeremy Waldron in 'Autonomy and Perfectionism in Raz's *Morality of Freedom*' (1989) 62 *Southern California LR* 1098, at 1127–28. Waldron appears to have missed the point of the argument when he draws an analogy between personal autonomy and virtues such as courage and temperance, and then observes, correctly, that an act or a lifestyle which displays such virtues need not be better or worse overall just because it displays them. But the point that emerges from Raz's examples (and mine) is that the autonomous choice of bad options *is* in fact morally *worse* than the non-autonomous choice of bad options, and worse precisely because it is an autonomous choice. (For Raz's reply see 'Facing Up: A Reply' (1989) 62 *Southern California LR* 1153, at 1228, n 160.) Waldron in turn outlines an alternative argument to the effect that the value of personal autonomy depends on the value of what is chosen autonomously, an argument that hinges on the premise that an autonomous choice is a choice for a reason, and that 'when people pursue goals they think valuable but which are not, then their well-being would be better promoted if they fail in their pursuit than if they succeeded.' This may be correct, yet the effect on well-being of success or failure in a misguidedly chosen pursuit need not correspond to whether or not the choice was made autonomously, and inasmuch as it does, this can only be the outcome of, not the explanation for, the dependency of the value of personal autonomy on the value of its exercise.

to do so with an eye on legal reality, that is the familiar and mostly justifiable ways in which freedom of contract is encroached upon in modern legal systems. Now earlier, in rejecting the argument according to which autonomy would be best enhanced if bad options were invariably left open for people to avoid *out of free choice*, I alluded to the fact that *some* bad options are bound to remain. This is probably enough to rebut the current objection. Yet in the current juncture it is worth considering again the typical circumstances for intervention in the freedom of contract—circumstances that render a general policy of leaving bad options open doubly ill-fated. These are circumstances where the choice of certain options, usually self-serving, by one party (usually the one with superior bargaining power) would have *harsh* implications for the other party; or, as in the more clearly paternalistic cases of intervention, circumstances where it is *particularly likely* that people would be tempted to choose the wrong option, and where such a choice would be liable to produce severe, rather than merely unpleasant or less than ideal, consequences. It would, I suspect, take a cynic to argue that concern for the autonomy-enhancing capacity to learn from mistakes recommends a general policy of non-interference in such cases.

By now it should be clear that what Atiyah aptly described as 'the whole trend of the law in the past fifty or even hundred years,' namely, 'greater protection for those who make rash and ill-considered promises,'[51] is, contrary to his contention, perfectly compatible with, and to a large extent required by, 'liberal principles'[52] in general, and the liberal commitment to promoting personal autonomy in particular. As I shall argue in the next section, differences between contract and promise lend this conclusion further support.

Autonomy, Contract and Promise

What I described as the starting point for the analysis of the relationship between the value of personal autonomy and freedom of contract, namely the notion that respect for personal autonomy recommends recognition of the binding force of voluntary undertakings of obligation, did not distinguish between contract and promise as two different types of voluntary undertaking. Indeed, the arguments which followed from that starting point appeared to be applicable to the same extent, and with the same limitations, to the freedom of contract and, to use an odd-sounding phrase, freedom of promise. This, as I shall now explain, is yet another sense in which the starting point was crude.

What bearing do the differences I highlighted between contract and promise have on the applicability of the value of personal autonomy to the issue at hand, freedom of contract? The answer is straightforward. The contrast between contract and promise in terms of intrinsic function and value entails that contracts, and hence freedom of contract, are simply not as significant for

[51] Above n 4, at 128.
[52] *Ibid.*

personal autonomy as are promises or freedom of promise. For an important part of what makes promises particularly significant for personal autonomy is the intrinsic function that they possess but contracts do not. The ability freely to create, develop, and mould relationships with others is an indispensable ingredient of personal autonomy. And the unique role that promises are capable of playing in this respect marks the practice out—and with it the freedom to partake in it—as conducive to autonomous life in a way which contracts, that do not typically fulfil a similar relationship-enhancing function, are not.

But what about the intrinsic function of contract, that of facilitating personal detachment? It could be pointed out in reply to my argument that the ability to maintain personal detachment should be as conducive to autonomy as the ability to develop personal relationships, especially given that (as we have seen) the value of personal detachment and the value of personal relationships tend to be mutually reinforcing. Yet this does not entail that minimal intervention in the freedom of contract would be as significant for personal autonomy as would a similar policy with regard to promise, and for reasons that are again related to the asymmetry between the respective intrinsic values of the two practices, asymmetry that has already surfaced in previous comparisons of the two. Personal relations are valuable regardless of the necessity to deal with other people. As a result promises, by virtue of their potential contribution to personal relations, can be valuable over and above their subject matter, or even when their subject matter is valueless. Personal detachment, by contrast, only has a distinct value where it is necessary to deal with others, or where some unwanted involvement with others is, for whatever reason, a distinct possibility. Thus personal detachment need only be protected or promoted as an option to dependence on personal relations for the pursuit of activities which are themselves valuable, or as a freedom from certain forms of involuntary and undesirable involvement with others. Contracts facilitate personal detachment in precisely these contexts: they enable people to deal with others while not depending on pre-existing personal relations with them and while not necessarily committing to creating such relations in future. And there is little point in enabling people to make through contracts, and thus *while maintaining personal detachment*, arrangements that we would not want them to make in any other way— arrangements that we would not want them to make at all. In such cases, the personal detachment that contracts facilitate is simply not valuable. This consideration suffices to buttress the conclusion towards which I have been driving, since legal intervention in the freedom of contract occurs mostly in cases where the arrangements that are struck down are considered undesirable as such, so that the point in striking them down is not merely to prevent them from being made *through contracting*, but rather to prevent them from being made altogether.

Conclusion

While concern for personal autonomy can lend basic support to the ideal of freedom of contract, it does not entail anything like the extreme conception of this ideal which is often associated with liberalism; neither does commitment to neutrality, inasmuch as such commitment is understood to be part and parcel of modern liberalism. The emerging picture is of liberalism as compatible with, and often positively requiring, various forms of intervention in the freedom of contract. Far from suggesting that the state must assume a 'stand off' stance, the liberal approach as delineated here assigns to the state a considerable role in shaping and regulating contractual activity. It requires the state to assume an active role in shaping the arena within which freedom of contract can be exercised, so as to ensure that by and large this freedom would enhance the well-being of those who enjoy it, and make a positive contribution to their chances of leading valuable, successful lives. The way in which legal systems throughout the industrialised world have been moving in this general direction, introducing measures designed to prevent contractual activity and the institutions that support it from serving as an instrument of exploitative or otherwise objectionable pursuits, and using contract law to foster various commercial, social, and moral standards, can probably be taken as evidence for the declining popularity of extreme philosophical individualism and related political doctrines. At the same time, such legal developments are as powerful an evidence for the growing eminence of the (non-individualistic, perfectionist) liberal approach, with its inherent commitment to promoting the conditions of autonomy, as a frame of reference in which to develop policies of government in general, and policies pertaining to contractual activity in particular.

II. FREEDOM FROM CONTRACT

Liberal theory is often said to encompasses two distinct conceptions of freedom: positive and negative, freedom *to* and freedom *from*.[53] The main issue of positive freedom arising around contract theory, namely the value and appropriate scope of the freedom of contract, was discussed in the first part of this chapter. Now, when it comes to negative freedom, the freedom *from* things, the first question arising would be from what exactly. Quite naturally, the emphasis in discussions of negative freedom has always been on freedom from coercion. At least in the context of liberal thought, the value and appropriate scope of

---

[53] For the classic formulation see I Berlin, 'Two Concepts of Liberty' (1958), reprinted in *Four Essays on Liberty* (Oxford, 1969). For a critique of the distinction see GC MacCallum Jr, 'Negative and Positive Freedom' (1967), reprinted in D Miller (ed), *Liberty* (Oxford, 1991) 100. For an account of the conceptual link between negative and positive freedom, see Raz, *The Morality of Freedom*, above n 22, at 409–10.

freedom from coercion is indeed a highly familiar theme: after all, it is the very notion that freedom from coercion is distinctly valuable that underlies the assumption that the use of coercion requires a special justification, and that begat doctrines such as Mill's harm principle.

Freedom from contract, an idea I wish to discuss now, could perhaps be construed as a private case of freedom from coercion: making a contract, and especially breaking a contract, can lead (at the end of a certain chain of events) to subjection to coercive measures, or at any rate (at the end of a shorter chain) to subjection to the adjudicating and enforcing authority of agencies that notably possess coercive powers. Yet there is no need to dwell on the potentially coercive implications of contractual relations in order to consider the proposition that freedom from contract may be of value or significance. Negative freedoms can sometimes be meaningful even in cases where coercion is not at all an issue, or at any rate not the main issue. For instance, people may have reasons to value the freedom from association with or involvement in various institutions and relations which do not possess and do not normally lead to the operation of coercive powers. In fact we have already come across a related idea in our discussion of the intrinsic value of contract. Indeed, this value will be at the centre of the discussion to follow.

The association at stake here is with the law; the relations at stake are legal relations. The question I wish to address arises directly out of the analogy between contract and promise. Both in promise-making and in making contracts people do a similar thing: they (voluntarily) undertake obligations to others. And the question is whether or to what extent people who make or exchange promises should enjoy the freedom from being considered as having established legal—contractual—relations.

As with every case of arguing in favour of a protected political or legal right to enjoy a negative freedom, the argument has to establish (for a start) that the freedom in question is of distinct value, that there is some benefit to be had from enjoying it and some ground for expecting the state to recognise and protect it. In what follows I wish to comment on the value of the freedom from contract, and on one or two of its normative and practical implications. Mainly for reasons of convenience (although a touch of realism should always be welcome) I will construct my comments around an existing, albeit much neglected, contract law doctrine: the requirement of an intention to create legal relations.[54]

Intention to Create Legal Relations

As textbooks uniformly inform us, 'an intention to create legal relations . . . is recognised by English law as *a separate requirement* for the formation of contracts.'[55] And yet, in contrast to the rather extensive treatment that the various

---

[54] See generally above n 13, at 149–60.
[55] *Ibid* at 160 (emphasis added).

'physical' formation requirements usually receive, textbooks and theoretical accounts alike tend to dedicate very little attention to the intention requirement.[56] As far as textbooks are concerned, the main explanation for this neglect is probably the relatively little attention that the intention requirement receives in courts, itself the result of the casual (and, in the most common types of contractual dispute, largely justified) use of factual presumptions (to the effect that the requisite intention was present), coupled with obvious evidential difficulties.[57] When it comes to theoretical accounts, however, the neglect may be owed to more substantial considerations.

In the framework of 'contract as promise' theories in particular, the requirement of an intention to create legal relations appears to be rather trivial, if not altogether superfluous. For the 'separate requirement' of an intention to create legal relations to be significant or even explicable, it should be possible to think of a reason why not to have such an intention in the relevant circumstances, or at least why not to ascribe it systematically to rational agents (in these circumstances) even allowing that they may not have actively or consciously entertained it. (When someone starts crossing the road, for instance, we can normally ascribe to her the intention to reach the other side of the road safely, regardless of whether or not we think that she is actively or consciously entertaining a specific thought to this effect.[58]) And if it is thought that there is no pertinent difference between contractual and promissory relations, and even more so if the former are thought to be but an improved version of the latter—if contracts are understood to offer all the benefits of promises (or exchanges of promises) with the additional bonus of enforceability—then the chances of finding such reasons look rather slim.

With one exception, of course. A party who is not sufficiently serious, sincere, or clear about the obligation she is undertaking, would understandably prefer (or should prefer) the undertaking not to be legally binding. With such cases in mind, and in the context of 'contract as promise' theories, the intention requirement can simply be understood as one way of making sure that the obligation in question was undertaken sincerely, seriously, or indeed intentionally at all. Thus understood, however, the intention requirement is rather trivial indeed. Obligations that have not been undertaken seriously or sincerely

---

[56] In Fried's *Contract as Promise* (above n 41), for instance, the intention to create legal relations is mentioned only once, in a footnote, in a chapter dedicated to the doctrine of consideration (at 38n).

[57] In the context of standard commercial relations, an intention to create legal relations is habitually (and sensibly) ascribed to the parties, and is rarely contested; and a party who wishes to contest it has the difficult onus of proving that no such intention existed. See above n 13, at 157–59.

[58] In his brief mention of the intention to create legal relations, Fried writes that '[t]he term as it stands is misleading. No one supposes that two merchants who make a deal must entertain some additional intention to create legal relations in order for that deal to be binding in law' (above n 41, at 38n). Yet the second part of this claim may be true precisely in light of the fact that in the context of a deal made by two merchants, the failure to entertain such an 'additional intention' is compatible with the assumption that the legal validity of the deal is in fact taken for granted by all parties— in which case there is nothing misleading about the term. See also Treitel, above n 13, at 157–59.

may sometimes be the subject of protective legal doctrines such as promissory estoppel or estoppel by representation, but are clearly not the normal case of making contracts, nor the normal case of promising. Similarly, people who are not entirely clear about what they are doing cannot normally be described as voluntarily undertaking an obligation of whatever kind, legal or non-legal. The 'intention to create' requirement, in other words, pertains, under this interpretation, to the act of undertaking an obligation as such, and not to the distinct *legal* nature of the obligation; the seriousness it demands is seriousness about entering a binding agreement per se, with the intention to create *legal* relations accounted for as but an inevitable implication thereof.[59]

The approach to contract I outlined in this work offers another way of ascribing significance to the intention requirement—a way which takes it to be a distinct condition, distinguishable from insisting on the seriousness or voluntariness of the undertaking of an obligation as such. With its account of the difference in terms of intrinsic function and value between contract and promise, and with the ensuing notion that there is something to lose, and not just gain, in opting for legal rather than non-legal relations, this theory allows for an understanding of the contractual intention requirement as a reminder that the scope for voluntariness or seriousness in making a contract may not be exhausted by the voluntariness or seriousness which is required in the context of exchanging promises. It recommends an understanding of the contractual intention requirement as stipulating that making a *legally binding* agreement should be voluntary; that the parties must be serious not just about undertaking an obligation, but about undertaking a legal obligation. For this theory comfortably accommodates the possibility that a person may be perfectly serious about doing the former, while not at all intending to do the latter: in (seriously, voluntarily) making agreements with others, people may opt not to enjoy the kind of reassurance that only the law can provide, in order not to lose the qualities which are often lost in the transition from non-legal to legal relations. They may wish to leave more room for the operation—and the transparency—of the 'right' motives. They may think it worthwhile to sacrifice some confidence (inasmuch as added confidence is felt to be significant or even possible in the circumstances) for the sake of enhancing personal trust, knocking down barriers to potential closeness, increasing the likelihood of developing personal bonds, or reinforcing existing ones. And it should be appreciated that such a preference need not make sense only where the subject matter of the agreement at stake or the circumstances surrounding it are distinctly private or intimate by nature,[60] or where

---

[59] If I understand him correctly, this is precisely the way Fried interprets the requirement of an intention to create legal relations. He mentions it as the term by which the law captures the qualification that '[t]he promisor must have been serious enough that subsequent legal enforcement was an aspect of what he should have contemplated at the time he promised' (above n 41, at 38n).

[60] Such cases are in fact largely recognised by the law as an exception for the purposes of applying the requirement of an intention to create legal relations. See 'Social and Domestic Arrangements' above n 13, at 151–53.

parties have some unique ideological stance that militates against entering the legal framework. To varying degrees of likelihood and intensity, the preference not to sacrifice the qualities that the legal framework tends to compromise may be pertinent in all circumstances of making agreements.

Patricia J Williams, in her book *The Alchemy of Race and Rights*,[61] provides a vivid illustration for such a preference in a beautifully told anecdote comparing the experiences of two protagonists engaged in apartment-hunting in New York. One of the protagonists ends up concluding a lease deal informally—deposit in cash, no lease, no receipt—saying that 'he didn't need to sign a lease because it imposed too much formality. The hand-shake and the good vibes were for him indicators of trust more binding than a form contract.' In the circumstances, this seemed the best strategy for him to adopt in order to 'establish enduring relationships with the [landlords], . . . to enhance trust . . . and to allow whatever closeness was possible.'[62]

I will want to return to this anecdote's second protagonist later. For now, we can see how, from my explanation of the possible rationale behind the preference not to establish *legal* relations, a justification emerges for why such a preference should, as a matter of legal policy, be allowed. Precisely because something valuable may be lost, and not just gained, in establishing relations within the legal framework, the option of staying outside it—the ability to exchange promises or make agreements with others without necessarily being 'captured' by the legal version of this practice—emerges as a meaningful freedom. It emerges as a negative freedom that serves a very significant kind of positive freedom: the freedom to develop and reinforce personal relationships through exchanging promises, or in other words the freedom to make use and enjoy the benefits of the intrinsic function of promise.

Of course, a fraudulent or a manipulative use of this negative freedom need not be allowed. A legal policy that sets out to protect it must still guard, for instance, against its cynical use as an easy way out of a regretted deal. But little seems to militate against a policy of allowing people to enjoy the freedom from contract in an honest way, in their activity within the legitimate bounds of the freedom of contract—or, as may be more appropriate here, the freedom of agreement.

The normative argument of the last paragraph may be valid from the perspective of one creed of political morality but not of others. What should be clear, however, is how naturally the freedom from contract fits with the liberal approach. We have seen that by allowing more scope for people to utilise the intrinsic function of promise, the freedom from contract is conducive to the pursuit of personal relationships. Thus it serves one of the central aspects of personal autonomy. The link to personal autonomy, however, is even stronger than this. For earlier we have also seen that the contrasting intrinsic functions of promises (enhancing personal relations) and contracts (promoting personal

[61] Cambridge, Massachusetts, 1991.
[62] *Ibid* at 146–47.

detachment) are both valuable for autonomy, and moreover that the value of personal relations and the value of personal detachment tend to be mutually-reinforcing when the ability to maintain detachment and the ability to have relationships co-exist as viable options in people's lives. Allowing people to enjoy the freedom from contract is one way of safeguarding the availability of this very option. And as a policy that helps sustain the conditions in which two autonomy-enhancing values reinforce each other, its place in a liberal frame of reference should be secure.

As I have hinted already, the practical legal implications of respect for the freedom from contract must not be exaggerated. As far as rules of evidence are concerned, for instance, the argument thus far need not be understood as advocating a radical departure from existing practices. Particularly when it comes to standard commercial transactions, employing the presumption that parties have intended to create legal relations,[63] and asking the party who claims otherwise to satisfy the relevant burden of proof, seems to me to be a perfectly sensible approach;[64] and in other contexts, more lenient rules of evidence already apply, and the presumption that the parties intended to create legal relations is employed more carefully, or not at all.[65]

More substantially, it should be noted that the argument in support of respect for the freedom from contract does not entail that parties to agreements (or receivers of promises) that were not intended to be legally binding should never be entitled to any kind of legal protection. A person who suffers loss as a result of honest reliance on an unjustifiably-broken promise should, in principle and in the right circumstances, be able to have her loss recovered. In the absence of an intention to create contractual relations—and hence in the absence of a contract—she would not be entitled to contractual remedies as such; but while performance remedies may, as a result, be excluded, nothing I said here militates against the award, possibly in tort, of (the equivalent of) reliance damages, to redress the actual loss. This suggestion should not be seen as incompatible with the preceding argument or with the tenor of this work in general, nor seen as remarkable in any other sense. Just as contractual relations are not the only source of liability for harm caused to others in general, likewise there is no reason to see such relations as the only possible source of liability for harm caused through an unjustified failure to discharge a voluntarily undertaken obligation. Only those who (like Atiyah) think that contractual obligations arise strictly out of reliance or that reliance damages should be the standard response to a breach of contract, are likely to see the possibility of awarding such damages *in the absence of a contract* as mounting some distinct theoretical challenge; and only

[63] Usually in cases of express, rather than merely implied, agreements; see above n 13, at 157–59. Drawing this distinction (ie between implied and express agreements) for the purposes of addressing the requirement of contractual intention is itself another practice which my argument does not necessarily challenge.
[64] See above n 57, and my comment in above n 58.
[65] See eg above n 60.

those who (like Fried) fail to recognise the differences between contract and promise—and therefore the significance of the contractual intention requirement—are likely to struggle in explaining the award of *no more* than reliance damages *despite the presence of an agreement.*

My argument concerning the freedom from contract may have a bearing on an issue we encountered briefly in Chapter 3, namely relational contracts. We saw that it is a typical feature of such contracts that over time, understandings and practices tend to develop between their parties that go beyond, or at any rate are different from, the terms of the contract that constituted the relationship in the first place. One of the most intricate problems arising in this area is whether and to what extent practices and understandings that so develop outside or around the contract can feed back into the legally binding agreement, supplementing or (perhaps more problematically) modifying its express terms in the process. Now by saying that the argument concerning the freedom from contract could have a bearing on the issue, I did not mean to suggest that it provides an answer to the problem. Rather, the argument indicates that there are no easy answers. For just as it need not be assumed in general that people who make agreements invariably intend to create legal relations, so it need not be assumed that explicit or implicit agreements that evolve around an existing contract are always intended to enter and become part of the legally binding arrangement. Those legitimate reasons for which people may wish not to bind themselves legally in the broader context of making agreements, along with the related reasons for allowing them (within limits) to have this wish respected, may apply in the particular context of relational contracts just the same.[66]

At this point let me return to Patricia Williams' apartment-hunting anecdote. We saw that the actions of its first protagonist—who is, I should now add, a white, male lawyer—illustrated the possibility and the possible merits of a preference to enter a binding and yet non-legal agreement. But the anecdote presses home yet another point, one that hints at the often greater complexities involved in choosing a strategy for making an agreement. For its second protagonist, Patricia Williams herself—also a lawyer, but black and female—the strategy of eschewing legal formalities did not seem viable. Despite the 'similarity of desire' between her and her white, male colleague, the only option open to her in the circumstances was to deal 'at arm's length,' speak 'the language of lease,' and make a formal contract.[67]

---

[66] The practical implications this argument may have in the particular context of practices which evolve around an exiting contract again need not be different from its implications in general. Thus, for instance, my argument does not imply that a party who suffers some loss as a result of a sudden withdrawal from such a practice by her counterpart (and where the practice in question is judged, possibly for lack of the required contractual intention, not to have become legally binding) should never enjoy any kind of legal protection. If, for example, the circumstances are such that her reliance on the continuation of the practice is thought to have been reasonable, and that the other party has acted unreasonably or irresponsibly (could or should have foreseen the reliance and the loss, could have easily prevented it, has not acted in good faith or exercised due care, etc), her loss in reliance should be recoverable, even though she would not be entitled to contractual remedies as such.

[67] Above n 61, at 147–48.

For current purposes, I think we can draw several distinct (though not unrelated) lessons from this part of the anecdote. First, it simply serves as a reminder of those differences between contract and promise that have been one of the main themes of this work. It illustrates how contract can serve as a genuine substitute for promise when it comes to these practices' similar instrumental functions. Indeed, as far as renting the apartment is concerned, it could be said that contract, unreliant (or anyway less reliant) on personal relationship and trust as it is, saved the day: it provided the only framework in which this particular tenant and these particular landlords could strike a mutually-advantageous deal. Yet when it comes to the intrinsic function that contract, as a practice, fulfils, this part of the anecdote illustrates yet another point that has emerged in earlier discussions. For the striking feature of the comparison between the two protagonists' experiences is not that one sought relationship and the other detachment; it is that one had the choice whereas the other did not. And the case of the latter illustrates the notion that personal detachment and personal relationships are valuable, and at that mutually-reinforcing, particularly when they co-exist as options in people's lives. The second protagonist's case illustrates that *dependence* on personal detachment is itself not so much a thing of value but a predicament. In this respect, there is a symmetry (alongside the various asymmetries I commented upon earlier) between personal relationship and personal detachment. When a person depends on one or the other for the realisation of any given goal, naturally she is better off having it than not having it—when a black woman needs to rent an apartment from (presumably) white, racist, sexist (or any combination thereof) landlords, she is better off having rather than not having the option of dealing at arm's length—but real value becomes a prospect particularly inasmuch as and to the extent that one-dimensional dependence is replaced by the freedom that comes with choice.

Bibliography

ATIYAH, Patrick S, *The Rise and Fall of Freedom of Contract* (Oxford, 1979).
—— *Promises, Morals, and Law* (Oxford, 1981).
—— *Essays on Contract* (Oxford, 1986).
AUSTIN, JL, *How to Do Things with Words* (2nd edn, Oxford, 1975).
BEALE, Hugh, 'Legislative Control of Fairness: The Directive on Unfair Terms in Consumer Contracts' in J Beatson and D Friedmann (eds), *Good Faith and Fault in Contract Law* (Oxford, 1995).
BEATSON, Jack and Friedmann, Daniel (eds), *Good Faith and Fault in Contract Law* (Oxford, 1995).
BENSON, Peter (ed), *The Theory of Contract: New Essays* (Cambridge, 2001).
BERLIN, Isaiah, *Four Essays on Liberty* (Oxford, 1969).
BRIDGE, Michael G, 'Mitigation of Damages in Contract and the Meaning of Avoidable Loss' (1989) 105 *Law Quarterly Review* 398.
BROWN, Harold I, *Rationality* (London and New York, 1988).
CAMPBELL, David, 'Ian Macneil and the Relational Theory of Contract' in D Campbell (ed), *The Relational Theory of Contract: Selected Works of Ian Macneil* (London, 2001) 3.
CARTER, WR, 'On Promising the Unwanted' (1972/3), 33 *Analysis* 88.
COHEN, Gerald A, 'Capitalism, Freedom, and the Proletariat' in D Miller (ed), *Liberty* (Oxford, 1991).
COLEMAN, Jules L, *Risks and Wrongs* (Cambridge, 1992).
COLLINS, Hugh, *Regulating Contracts* (Oxford, 1999).
CRASWELL, Richard, 'Contract Law, Default Rules, and the Philosophy of Promising' (1989) 88 *Michigan Law Review* 489.
DAN-COHEN, Meir, 'In Defence of Defiance' (1994) 23 *Philosophy and Public Affairs* 24.
DE MOOR, Anne, 'Are Contracts Promises' in J Eakelaar and J Bell (eds), *Oxford Essays in Jurisprudence* (3rd Series, Oxford, 1987).
EISENBERG, Melvin A, 'Relational Contracts' in J Beatson and D Friedmann (eds), *Good Faith and Fault in Contract Law* (Oxford, 1995) 291.
FEINBERG, Joel, *Harm to Others* (Oxford, 1984).
FEINMAN, Jay, 'The Reception of Ian Macneil's Work on Contract in the USA' in D Campbell (ed), *The Relational Theory of Contract: Selected Works of Ian Macneil* (London, 2001) 59.
FINNIS, John M, *Natural Law and Natural Rights* (Oxford, 1980).
FREEDEN, Michael, *Ideologies and Political Theory: A Conceptual Approach* (Oxford, 1997).
FRIED, Charles, *Right and Wrong* (Cambridge, Massachusetts, 1978).
—— *Contract as Promise: A Theory of Contractual Obligation* (Cambridge, Massachusetts, 1981).
FRIEDMANN, Daniel, 'The Efficient Breach Fallacy' (1989) 18 *Journal of Legal Studies* 1.
—— 'The Performance Interest in Contract Damages' (1995) 111 *Law Quarterly Review* 628.

FULLER, Lon, *The Principles of Social Order* (Durham, North Carolina, 1981).

—— and Perdue, Will, 'The Reliance Interest in Contract Damages' (1936/37) 46 *Yale Law Journal* 52, at 373.

GANS, Chaim, *Philosophical Anarchism and Political Disobedience* (Cambridge, 1992).

GILMORE, Grant, *The Death of Contract* (Columbus, 1974).

GOETZ, Charles J and Scott, Robert E, 'Principles of Relational Contract' (1981) 67 *Virginia Law Review* 1089.

GRAY, John, *Mill on Liberty: A Defence* (2nd edn, London, 1996).

GREEN, TH, *Lectures on the Principles of Political Obligation and Other Writing* (P Harris and J Morrow (eds), Cambridge ,1986).

GRIFFITHS, M, *Law for Purchasing and Supply* (2nd edn, London, 1996).

HART, Herbert LA, *The Concept of Law* (Oxford, 1961).

HOLMES, Oliver Wendell, *The Common Law* (Boston, 1881).

KENNEDY, Duncan, 'Form and Substance in Private Law Adjudication' (1976) 89 *Harvard Law Review* 1685.

KRAUS, Jody S, 'Philosophy of Contract Law' in J Coleman and S Shapiro (eds), *The Oxford Handbook of Jurisprudence and Philosophy of Law* (Oxford, 2002) 687.

KRONMAN, Anthony T, 'Paternalism and the Law of Contract' (1983) 92 *Yale Law Journal* 763.

LEWIS, David K, *Convention* (Cambridge, Massachusetts, 1969).

LOCKE, Don, 'The Object of Morality, and the Obligation to Keep a Promise' (1972) 2 *Canadian Journal of Philosophy* 135.

LYONS, David, *Rights, Welfare, and Mill's Moral Theory* (Oxford, 1994).

MACCORMICK, Neil, 'Voluntary Obligations and Normative Powers' (1972) Supp vol 46 *Proceedings of the Aristotelian Society* 59.

MACNEIL, Ian, 'The Many Futures of Contract' (1974) 47 *Southern California Law Review* 691.

—— 'Essays on the Nature of Contracts' (1980) 10 *Southern Carolina Central Law Journal* 159.

—— 'Economic Analysis of Contractual Relations' (1981) 75 *Northwestern University Law Review* 1018.

—— *The Relational Theory of Contract: Selected Works of Ian Macneil* (D Campbell (ed), London, 2001).

MARMOR, Andrei, 'On Convention' (1996) 107 *Synthese* 349.

MCKENDRICK, Ewan, 'The Regulation of Long-Term Contracts in English Law' in J Beatson and D Friedmann (eds), *Good Faith and Fault in Contract Law* (Oxford, 1995) 305.

MILL, John Stuart, *On Liberty and Other Essays* (Oxford World's Classics edn, Oxford, 1998).

MILLER, David (ed), *Liberty* (Oxford, 1991).

MONTEFIORE, Alan (ed), *Neutrality and Impartiality* (Cambridge, 1975).

NOZICK, Robert, 'Coercion' in P Laslett, WG Runciman and Q Skinner (eds), *Philosophy, Politics, and Society* (4th series, Oxford, 1972).

—— *Anarchy, State, and Utopia* (New York, 1974).

PENNER, James E, 'Voluntary Obligations and the Scope of the Law of Contract' (1996) 2 *Legal Theory* 325.

POLLOCK, Frederick, *Principles of Contract* (3rd edn, London, 1881).

RAWLS, John, *A Theory of Justice* (Cambridge, Massachusetts, 1971).
—— *Political Liberalism* (New York, 1993)
RAZ, Joseph, 'Voluntary Obligations' (1972) Supp vol 46 *Proceedings of the Aristotelian Society* 79.
—— 'Promises and Obligations' in PMS Hacker and J Raz (eds), *Law, Morality and Society* (Oxford, 1977).
—— *The Authority of Law* (Oxford, 1979).
—— 'Book Review: Promises in Morality and Law' (1982) 95 *Harvard Law Review* 916.
—— *The Morality of Freedom* (Oxford, 1986).
—— 'Facing Up: A Reply' (1989) 62 *Southern California LR* 1153.
—— 'Liberty and Trust' in RP George (ed), *Natural Law, Liberalism, and Morality* (Oxford, 1996).
—— *Practical Reason and Norms* (2nd edn, Princeton, 1990).
SCANLON, Thomas M, 'Promises and Practices' (1990) 19 *Philosophy and Public Affairs* 199.
—— *What We Owe to Each Other* (Cambridge, Massachusetts, 1998).
—— 'Promises and Contracts' in P Benson (ed), *The Theory of Contract: New Essays* (Cambridge, 2001) 86.
SCHEFFLER, Samuel, *Human Morality* (Oxford, 1992).
—— *Boundaries and Allegiances: Problems of Justice and Responsibility in Liberal Thought* (Oxford, 2001).
SCHWARTZ, Alan, 'The Case for Specific Performance' (1979) 89 *Yale Law Journal* 271.
—— 'Relational Contracts in the Courts: An Analysis of Incomplete Agreements and Judicial Strategies' (1992) 21 *Journal of Legal Studies* 21.
SEARLE, John, *Speech Acts* (Cambridge, 1969).
SMITH, LD, 'Disgorgement of the Profits of Breach of Contract' (1994–95) 24 *Can Bus LJ* 121.
SMITH, Stephen A, 'Performance, Punishment, and the Nature of Contractual Obligation' (1997) 60 *Modern Law Review* 360.
TREBILCOCK, Michael, *The Limits of Freedom of Contract* (Cambridge, Massachusetts, 1993).
TREITEL, GH, *Remedies for Breach of Contract: A Comparative Account* (Oxford, 1988).
—— *The Law of Contract* (10th edn, London, 1999).
VINCENT-JONES, Peter, 'The Reception of Ian Macneil's Work on Contract in the U.K.' in D Campbell (ed), *The Relational Theory of Contract: Selected Works of Ian Macneil* (London, 2001) 67.
WALDRON, Jeremy, 'Autonomy and Perfectionism in Raz's *Morality of Freedom*' (1989) 62 *Southern California LR* 1098.
WARNOCK, GJ, *The Object of Morality* (London, 1971).
WILLIAMS, Bernard, *Ethics and the Limits of Philosophy* (Cambridge, Massachusetts, 1985).
WILLIAMS, Patricia J, *The Alchemy of Race and Rights* (Cambridge, Massachusetts, 1991).

Index